LATIN

A Fresh Approach Book 1

MIKE SEIGEL

Anthem Press
An imprint of Wimbledon Publishing Company
www.anthempress.com

This edition first published in UK and USA 1999
by ANTHEM PRESS
75-76 Blackfriars Road, London SE1 8HA, UK
or PO Box 9779, London SW19 7ZG, UK
and
244 Madison Ave. #116, New York, NY 10016, USA

British Library Cataloguing in Publication Data
A catalogue record for this book is available from the British Library.

Library of Congress Cataloging in Publication Data
A catalog record for this book has been requested.

Illustrated by A. Harrison

1 3 5 7 9 10 8 6 4 2

ISBN–10: 1 89885 525 0 (Pbk)
ISBN–13: 978 1 89885 525 5 (Pbk)

Cover design: PM Graphics

Printed in India

MIKE SEIGEL

Mike Seigel has had a distinguished academic and teaching career. An Oxford University graduate, he won an Exhibition to New College where he read Classics. After joining St Paul's School and Colet Court in 1973, Mike was Head of Classics at Colet Court from 1976 to 1987, during which period more than 80 of his pupils succeeded in getting scholarships to the most prestigious Independent schools in the UK, including Eton, St Paul's, Winchester and Westminster. He then concentrated his teaching on GCSE and A level classes, as well as working as a Careers and Universities Adviser, before being appointed Headmaster of Rokeby School, Kingston-upon-Thames.

FOR

Wendy, Emma and Alexander

*and all my pupils
past, present and future*

Acknowledgements

The author and publishers are grateful to the following for permission to reproduce copyright material and illustrations:

David Camden, Leo Curran, the BBC, Barnaby's Picture Gallery, Paula Chabot, Leslie Noles, the European Community, the Ancient Sites website, Ronald Embleton, Mark Hegarty, the U.S. National Archives and Records Administration, Dr Peter Wade-Martin of the Norfolk Museum Service, R.L. Dalladay, Christopher Wood, F. Trefeu and the NCMA.

Every effort has been made to contact all copyright holders before publication. If there are any omissions the publishers will be pleased to rectify them at the earliest opportunity.

We are most grateful to all those people who sent in constructive comments after they had seen the uncorrected book proof, and several of their helpful suggestions have been included in this final version.

Particular thanks are due to the following for their kind and helpful input: John Hazel, John Traupman, William Harris, Paul Tweddle and especially John Smith.

Introduction

This book is the first of three volumes, which will form a complete beginner's course to bring pupils up to the level which starts my previous book *Latin: From Common Entrance to GCSE.*

Those familiar with my previous book will recognise a similar style here.

I have tried to combine clarity of explanation with a somewhat more traditional approach. The aim is very much to make the basics of the Latin language easy and accessible to pupils, whatever their age, as they embark on what I trust will be a satisfying study of the subject.

I hope that the layout and explanation of the grammar will facilitate the learning process. The pace is deliberately slow and steady: my thoughts have been that this book will be used for the whole of a student's first year of Latin, but for older pupils the pace could easily be accelerated.

There is deliberately no continuous story in Latin, but instead plenty of linguistic exercises which it is hoped will give sufficient practice in emphasising the basic points, while allowing pupils time to gain confidence in understanding one new point before they move on to the next.

My intention is also to teach the language alongside the culture and civilisation which produced it. I have therefore made the introduction to the language very gradual in the first few chapters, and thereafter I provide background material in English at the end of each chapter.

This material is designed to be interesting and relevant for its own sake, but has also been compiled with the Common Entrance syllabus in mind, for those who are preparing for that exam. I have also provided exercises in this area to provide variety and to inspire the pupils to pursue their own research on these topics.

Vocabulary has been introduced at regular intervals, and I have aimed to make the lists of manageable length so that they will be more easily learnt. I have also tried to use all new words in the various exercises to aid recognition and memory of their meaning. Here too I have had the Common Entrance syllabus in mind, but have widened the vocabulary a little to include words met in the "background" sections.

As with my previous book, I hope that this course will make the learning of Latin both stimulating and enjoyable!

Mike Seigel
June 1999

Contents

Lions and other wild beasts from all over the Roman Empire were used as entertainment. In this picture, Christians in the Circus Maximus are awaiting the attack of lions and tigers. Picture courtesy of Barnaby's Picture Gallery.

WHY STUDY LATIN? 1

As we progress into the new millennium, you may well be asking yourself why you are about to study a language which was being spoken two thousand years ago! You may perhaps have heard the little poem which many schoolchildren have recited over the years:

> Latin is a language,
> As dead as dead can be.
> It killed the Ancient Romans,
> And now it's killing me.

Yet Latin is not truly dead: its very language and its influence live on, as you will discover further in Chapter 3. Not only does English owe so much of its vocabulary to Latin (the word **millennium** itself is from Latin, meaning 1000 years), but many of the modern languages which you may learn are derived directly from Latin, such as French, Italian and Spanish.

Studying Latin is more than just studying a language: it is not only the study of words, of vocabulary and grammar, but it is also the study of a civilisation which was enormously important in the ancient world, and which has left its mark on the history and culture of modern Europe.

Today we often hear discussion about co-operation within the European Union, and of linking our currencies and our politics. Britain has now been joined – thanks to the Channel Tunnel – to continental Europe for the first time since the Ice Age. Yet this move towards closer harmony is not really new – it does, in fact, go back to the days of the Roman Empire so many years ago.

A 'denarius' showing the head of Julius Caesar

Chapter 1

EXERCISE 1.1

Study the two maps very carefully: the first is of the Roman Empire in AD 250, the second is of Europe today. In the first you can see which countries were part of Rome's mighty empire, and which were not; in the second you see which countries are currently part of the EU and which are not.

1. Make a list of the countries included in each, and work out which ancient countries correspond to which modern ones.

2. Why do you think certain countries have been excluded from both?

3. How similar is the pattern between the two maps?

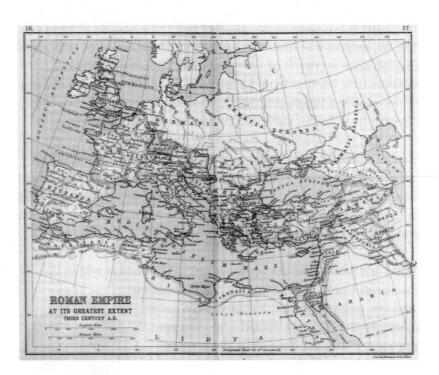

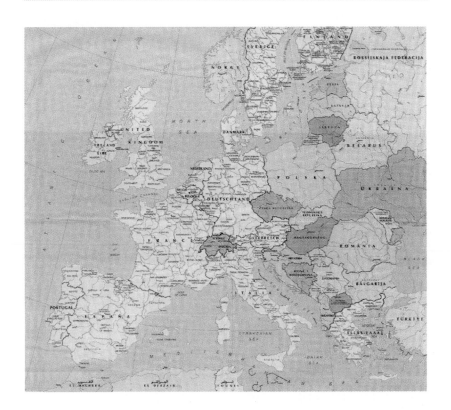

The Magna Carta is one of the most important documents ever written. It is an excellent example of the influence and importance that the Latin language has enjoyed throughout history. Picture courtesy of the United States National Archives and Records Administration.

AN OUTLINE OF ROMAN HISTORY 2

The civilisation for which Rome is famous did not, of course, spring up overnight. The mighty Roman Empire which you were looking at in the last chapter took several centuries to grow into the shape depicted in the map you were studying.

I wonder how many Romans you have heard of. In the previous chapter you saw a coin (a silver **denarius**) of **Julius Caesar.** He was the man who, when he tried to gain too much power, was murdered on the famous date of **the Ides of March.** This was 15 March, and the year was **44 BC**. This makes a useful central date for us to look both forward and backward across the Roman timescale.

Another very famous Roman you may have heard of is the emperor **Hadrian**, who built his historic wall in northern Britain. He lived more than 150 years after Julius Caesar, and he visited Britain in **AD 122**, when he made plans for the building of the wall, part of which survives to this day.

A section of Hadrian's Wall

You will read more about this in Chapter 13.

Chapter 2

Don't worry that you will need to learn a seemingly endless list of dates, but it is useful for you to realise just how long Rome's influence lasted. Rome began as a tiny city, perhaps founded – as legend tells us – by **Romulus and Remus** (see Chapter 15), over seven centuries before the birth of Christ, and the Roman Empire collapsed more than four centuries into the Christian Era. So you will see by simple arithmetic that Rome's history itself lasted for over a millennium.

Today, people often appear to think that Rome flourished a long time ago, but within only a short space of time. The first point may be true, but clearly the second is not. To Roman schoolchildren living at the time of Julius Caesar events of early Roman history – like the story of Romulus and Remus – seemed as remote to them as the Battle of Hastings does to us. Roman emperors did not actually start to reign until nearly twenty years after Caesar's death and then went on for nearly five hundred more years.

753 BC   Legendary founding of Rome

Rome ruled by Kings until:

509 BC   Rome is now a Republic

by 250 BC   Rome has control of central and southern Italy

by 100 BC   Rome has control of the Mediterranean area

54 BC   Caesar's invasion of Britain

44 BC   Murder of Julius Caesar

27 BC   Julius Caesar's adopted son becomes the first Emperor, taking the name Augustus

The Roman Empire in the West survives until:

AD 476   Last Emperor of Rome is deposed by Germanic tribes

The Eastern Roman Empire lasts until:

AD 1453   Fall of Constantinople

The dates above are simply to show something of the extent of Rome's history. There is a very great deal that you could learn about the many events of Rome's turbulent history over the centuries, perhaps at a later stage of your school career.

Have you thought how we know about Roman history? Some of our evidence comes from **archaeologists** who dig things up from under the ground. This is still going on today – in Italy and also in our own country – enabling us to find out more all the time about what life was really like for the Romans and the people that they ruled.

Most of our knowledge comes from what the Romans wrote themselves (in Latin, of course), and this is one of the reasons why people today still want to learn Latin – in order to be able to read first-hand about what happened so many centuries ago.

Julius Caesar, as well as being a general and a politician, was also a writer. It is from his own accounts that we know so much about his wars in Gaul and his expeditions to Britain (see Chapter 12). There were many other writers too, some of whom wrote history, others poetry or plays.

EXERCISE 2.1

1. When we read accounts of early Roman history written by the Romans centuries later should we believe every word they write?

2. Do you think modern historians might be more accurate when writing about events long ago than the Romans were? If so, why?

3. Julius Caesar was writing about events of his own time – his own victories in Gaul or Britain. Do you think his accounts are likely to be 100% accurate?

4. Do you think that newspaper accounts of what happens in the news today are always accurate?

The arch of Septimius Severus, which stands in the Forum in Rome.
To see what the Forum looked like in Roman times, see page 27.
Picture courtesy of Leo Curran.

THE LATIN LANGUAGE

3

You must not think that one day, a long time ago, a committee of nasty Romans sat down and decided to concoct a difficult language for schoolchildren to battle with centuries later! There was one language which was deliberately invented, over a hundred years ago; this was called Esperanto, but it was not a great success.

Latin didn't just happen – it evolved. This means that it gradually developed and kept on changing, just as English does. If you read some English written in Anglo-Saxon times (nearly 1500 years ago) you would think it a different language, and, if you read some of the poems Geoffrey Chaucer wrote about 600 years ago, you would find his language quite strange too.

The Latin that you will study is that written and spoken during the central period of Roman history – i.e. around the time of **Julius Caesar** (see last chapter). This is very different from the earliest writings which survive from some 500 or more years before his time. The Latin which comes down to us is

either that written on papyrus (the early form of books) or on stone like the inscription shown left.

An inscription from the tomb of Alpinus Classicianus, the procurator of the province of Britannia, who died in London around AD 65.

Towards the end of the Roman period Latin was changing again, partly because of time and partly because of distance. The Latin spoken in the province of **Hispania (Spain)** in, for example, AD 400 was rather different from that spoken in the province of Dacia (Romania). These different dialects of Latin gradually turned into what we today call the Romance languages, that is the languages which come from the Roman language of Latin.

These are: **Italian**
French
Spanish
Portuguese
Romanian

Look at the following list and note how similar the words are in the different languages which come from Latin and how similar they all are to the Latin:

	Latin	**Italian**	**Spanish**	**French**
(father)	**pater**	padre	padre	père
(mother)	**māter**	madre	madre	mère
(son)	**fīlius**	figlio	hijo	fils
(daughter)	**fīlia**	figlia	hija	fille
(friend)	**amīcus**	amico	amigo	ami
(water)	**aqua**	acqua	agua	eau
(wall)	**mūrus**	muro	muro	mur
(wine)	**vīnum**	vino	vino	vin

You can see from these examples how Latin did not simply stop, but stays alive in these modern languages. There are many other examples like this, and the numbers provide a particularly good way of seeing Latin evolve into the modern languages.

	Roman numbers	Latin	Italian	Spanish	French
1	I	**ūnus**	uno	uno	un
2	II	**duo**	due	dos	deux
3	III	**trēs**	tre	tres	trois
4	IV	**quattuor**	quattro	cuatro	quatre
5	V	**quīnque**	cinque	cinco	cinq
6	VI	**sex**	sei	seis	six
7	VII	**septem**	sette	siete	sept
8	VIII	**octō**	otto	ocho	huit
9	IX	**novem**	nove	nueve	neuf
10	X	**decem**	dieci	diez	dix

Here again you can easily see the similarities, and you must remember that Latin is the parent language of Italian, Spanish etc, when you come to pronounce it. Too many people try to pronounce Latin as though it were English!

Your teacher will help you with this, but it might be useful for you to bear in mind the following rules about certain

consonant sounds in Latin:

c is always a hard sound as in English **c**ap or **c**art

g is always a hard sound as in English **g**oat or **g**ate

gn is sounded as **ngn**: so magnus sounds ma**ngn**us

i there is a consonant **i** as well as a vowel **i**, and it is sounded like **y** in English: so iuvo sounds **y**uvo

s is always sounded as in English **s**au**s**age

v is sounded like **w** in English: so video sounds **w**ideo

With regard to the **vowel** sounds you must make them more rounded than in English, and if you already know some French, Italian or Spanish it will help.

Macrons (long vowel signs) have been placed on the appropriate vowels on words in this chapter, but for the sake of simplicity they will be used sparingly in this course – mainly to distinguish endings. It is important to try to pronounce Latin as authentically as possible, but this is of course an oral exercise, and experience shows that pupils are sometimes hindered rather than helped by seeing the macrons on the printed page.

Your teacher will help you with the vowel sounds, but the following guidelines may be useful:

a short as in English c**u**p (not cap)
ā long as in English f**a**ther
e short as in English m**e**t
ē long as in English m**ai**m
i short as in English b**i**t
ī long as in English b**ea**t
o short as in English g**o**t
ō long as in English g**oa**t
u short as in English f**oo**t
ū long as in English f**oo**l

Some vowels are written together to make one sound: these are called **diphthongs**.

ae as in English s**igh**
au as in English c**ow**
ei as in English **eight**
oe as in English b**oy**

EXERCISE 3.1

1. Take note of the points above about Latin pronunciation, and look again at both the list of Latin nouns above and the list of numbers 1 to 10. Then read them aloud, taking care to make them sound like Latin and not English!

2. Try to find somebody who knows some Portuguese or Romanian. Find out from them what the words are in those languages for the numbers 1 to 10 or for the words in the other list. See if they are also like Latin and the other Romance languages.

EXERCISE 3.2

Learn the Latin numbers from 1 to 10 and then do these simple sums and answer in Latin.

1. decem − sex =
2. duo + tres =
3. tres × tres =
4. quattuor × duo =
5. unus + septem − quinque =

EXERCISE 3.3

As was said at the start of the book, English owes a great deal of its vocabulary to Latin.

1. Use the meanings of the words in this chapter (and a dictionary, if necessary!) to find out the meanings of the following words:

    paternal   maternal   filial   aquatic   unicorn

2. The Latin numbers from seven to ten should remind you of four English months, which take their names directly from Latin. Write down the names of these four months. What do the meanings of these months tell us about when the Roman year started?

This is a funerary monument to a prominent Roman family. You can see the abbreviations of the names of the three people engraved into the stone: Sextus Maelius Stabilio, Vesinia Iucunda and Sextus Maelius Faustus. Picture courtesy of North Carolina Museum of Art.

ROMAN NAMES AND FAMILIES

4

In Chapter 2 you came across the famous Roman **Julius Caesar**, and you will read a little more about him later in this book. Julius Caesar is the name by which we know this well-known statesman and general, or sometimes we just call him **Caesar.**

However, most Romans had three names, and Julius Caesar's full name was **Gaius Julius Caesar.** The first name was the equivalent of our first name, the second was the original family name and the last was an additional name which the family had taken on in earlier times (often originally a nickname of one of them) to distinguish it from other branches of the same family.

The Latin word for name is **nomen**, and so this referred to the middle name. The forename is the **praenomen**, and the surname the **cognomen.**

So: **GAIUS   JULIUS   CAESAR**
           praenomen   nomen   cognomen

Today we often refer to famous Romans by just one name, like the poets **Virgil** and **Horace**, or the orator and politician **Cicero** who lived in the time of Julius Caesar. However, their full names were as follows:

Publius Vergilius Maro
Quintus Horatius Flaccus
Marcus Tullius Cicero

As you can see we are not consistent about their modern names: sometimes we adapt their **nomen** (like **Virgil** from Vergilius or **Horace** from Horatius) and sometimes we use their **cognomen** (like **Caesar** or **Cicero**).

Girls however were treated with less respect and formality. They usually had only one name and this was the female form of the family **nomen.** So Caesar's daughter was called **Julia** (from Julius) and Cicero's daughter was called **Tullia** (from Tullius).

Note that in Latin Julius and Julia were spelt with an initial **I**: **Iulius** and **Iulia** – this is the consonant i which was mentioned in the last chapter.

Today first names are many and varied, ranging from the more unusual like Cedric and Quentin through the more common John, David, Michael etc. to the likes of Wayne and Darren. Latin on the other hand had only a few first names, and these included the ones already mentioned: **Gaius, Marcus, Publius** and **Quintus.**

In the last chapter you were introduced to the Latin words for certain members of the family. Here is a family tree to help you remember the meaning of these words and a few more besides:

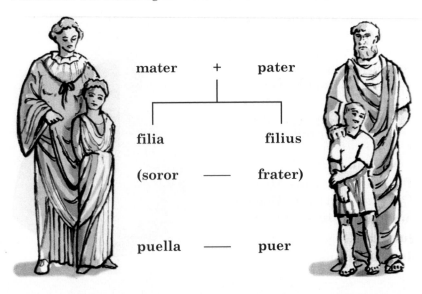

mater   +   pater

filia   filius

(soror   ——   frater)

puella   ——   puer

EXERCISE 4.1

1.   Study the diagram above, and see if you can deduce the meanings of **frater, soror, puer** and **puella.**
     (If not, there is always the vocabulary at the back, but only use this as a last resort!)

2.   With your parents' help make a family tree of your own and see how far back you can go.

EXERCISE 4.2

Revise your Latin numbers from the last chapter, and then do the following sums.

1.   octo − tres =
2.   septem + duo =
3.   quinque × duo =
4.   novem − quinque =
5.   unus + duo + tres =

This is what the Forum would have looked like in Roman times. Parts of the Forum, which was really the heart of the city, have survived, and you can see what it looks like today on page 13. Picture courtesy of Ancient Sites.

NOUNS AND VERBS: AN INTRODUCTION 5

In the previous two chapters we have met several nouns, both what we call **proper nouns** and **common nouns**.

Proper nouns are the names of actual people or places like **Michael, London** or **England**.

Common nouns are the words which name individual items, like **boy, city** or **country**.

Here are the **Latin proper nouns** which you have met so far:

Caesar	Gaius
Marcus	Publius
Quintus	Iulia
Tullia	

and the **common nouns:**

pater	father
mater	mother
filius	son
filia	daughter
frater	brother
soror	sister
puer	boy
puella	girl
nomen	name
amicus	friend
aqua	water
murus	wall
vinum	wine

Nouns on their own name somebody, but they do not tell us anything else about the person. If we want to know what a person is doing then we need to use a verb – consider the following examples:

The boy **is walking.**
The girl **is swimming.**

The words in bold tell us what the boy and the girl are doing, and the same is true in Latin, where the verbs describe the action.

EXERCISE 5.1

Look at the following pictures, and work out from them what each caption means.

puella ambulat

puer natat

mater cantat

pater laborat

Various points should be noticed about translating from Latin into English:

1) Latin does not use words for **"a"** or **"the"**. So

    puella can mean **"a girl"** or **"the girl"**

    and you have to decide which is better from the context.

2) Latin, like most modern languages, has only one form of the present tense – it is English which is the exception. So

    ambulat can mean **"walks"** or **"is walking"** or even **"does walk"**

    and again you have to decide which one seems best.

3) Latin only uses capital letters for proper names – unlike English, it does not use them to begin all sentences.

    Other verbs like those in the captions include:

aedificat	builds, is building
appropinquat	approaches, is approaching
clamat	shouts, is shouting
festinat	hurries, is hurrying
navigat	sails, is sailing
pugnat	fights, is fighting
stat	stands, is standing
vocat	calls, is calling
laborat	works, is working

EXERCISE 5.2

Translate into English.

1. pater appropinquat.
2. mater clamat.
3. puella vocat.
4. puer pugnat.
5. Gaius natat.

6. frater navigat.

7. soror cantat.

8. Caesar festinat.

9. Iulia stat.

10. Publius aedificat.

EXERCISE 5.3

Translate into Latin.

1. The boy is shouting.

2. The girl is working.

3. Gaius is walking.

4. The mother is calling.

5. The daughter is singing.

A further point should be noted about translating Latin verbs:

clamat can mean **"is shouting"** if it follows a noun.

e.g.	**puer clamat.**
means	The boy is shouting

But **clamat** can stand on its own and mean **"he is shouting"** or **"she is shouting"**.

Latin does have words for "he" or "she" but it does not use them, if the meaning is obvious.

So	**puer pugnat. clamat.**
means	The boy is fighting. He is shouting

EXERCISE 5.4

Translate into English.

1.   mater stat. vocat.
2.   puer appropinquat. festinat.
3.   Marcus natat. clamat.
4.   Tullia laborat. cantat.
5.   amicus ambulat. appropinquat.

EXERCISE 5.5

Translate into Latin.

1.   The girl is building. She is singing.
2.   The brother is sailing. He is calling.
3.   The boy is hurrying. He is shouting.
4.   Julia is swimming. She is calling.
5.   Gaius is working. He is hurrying.

Note the following important and common words:

> **et**   and
> **sed**   but
> **non**   not

e.g.   **puella ambulat et cantat.**
        The girl is walking and singing.

        puer non cantat.
        The boy is not singing.

EXERCISE 5.6

Translate into English.

1.   Quintus non festinat.
2.   puer vocat et clamat.
3.   filia ambulat et cantat.
4.   mater non ambulat, sed stat.
5.   puella non pugnat, sed aedificat.

EXERCISE 5.7

Translate into Latin.

1.   The sister is swimming and shouting.
2.   The brother is not working.
3.   The boy is not shouting.
4.   Julia is not fighting, but she is shouting.
5.   Marcus is not singing, but calling.

EXERCISE 5.8

From the new Latin words in this chapter try to work out the meanings of these English words:

> **clamour**
> **navigate**
> **laboratory**
> **perambulator**
> **puerile**
> **stationary**
> **vocation**

LIFE IN ANCIENT ROME

As was emphasised in Chapter 2, the period of Roman history went on for a very long time. Therefore, in 500 BC, for example, life was very different for people in the small town of Rome, growing up along the **river Tiber** and struggling against its hostile neighbours from what it was several centuries later in AD 150, for example, by which time Rome was ruler of a mighty empire.

So when we think about life in ancient Rome, as we shall in later chapters of this book, we must remember that it changed considerably and of course differed for different sorts of people: the rich and the poor, those living in the city, those who lived in the country, and those who lived in the various provinces of the far-flung empire (see map on p.4).

The same is of course true today. When we compare our lives to those of the ancient Romans, we no doubt think about how they did not have our modern conveniences like the car, the telephone, the television, the computer, the washing machine etc.

However, we must be careful when we make such comparisons, for even today in what we call the Third World (e.g. many countries of Africa, Asia and South America) there are countless people who do not have these things. For instance, did you know that more than half the people living in the world today have never used a telephone?

Boots such as these were common in Roman times. The style of these boots was worked out because of a print left in some drying cement in Caistor. Picture by David Fox.

Do not imagine that as the years and centuries roll forward there is a continuous line of progress for everyone. This is certainly not the case. In fact life in Rome in AD 150 was far more advanced and civilised for many than it was in lots of countries centuries later.

The city of Rome at this time was largely peaceful, and there was a modest police force and fire-fighting service. Life for the poor was not always pleasant, but there were those who lived very comfortably and some people even had central heating in their homes. We shall read more about this in the next chapter.

One of the several things that the ancient Romans lacked was a precise sense of time. In our lifestyle we have recently become obsessed by time. Trains leave at times like 10.58, video machines are set to record television programmes to start at 17.35, and athletes' speeds are measured in hundredths of seconds. This is all very well, but not very relaxing!

The Romans had no digital watches, but measured time by the sun, hourglasses, waterclocks or candles. Meetings would therefore be casual and approximate, and life would have a less urgent feel about it. You can see from this that perhaps not all "progress" is necessarily for the best.

EXERCISE 5.9

If you were transported in a time machine to ancient Rome, what things would you most miss about your current lifestyle? Are there any things which you think you might prefer about life in a different age or place?

This picture shows the peristylium of a Roman villa. This picture is from a model of the 'House of the Tragic Poet' in Pompeii. Photograph courtesy of R. Dalladay.

SUBJECT AND OBJECT

6

Consider the following English sentences:

> **He** likes **the girl.**
> **The girl** likes **him.**

Why do you think there is a different word for **he** and **him** in these two sentences?

The answer is that in the first sentence **he** is doing the liking, and we call that the **subject** of the sentence.

In the second **the girl** is doing the liking, and **him** becomes the **object** of the verb.

In English you will note that **the girl** stays the same, whether **Subject** or **Object**, because our nouns do not change. Very few English words do, but:

> **he** becomes **him**
> **she** becomes **her**
> **who** still sometimes becomes **whom**

In Latin, however, most nouns change their ending if they become the object of a sentence. Consider the following:

> **Gaius puellam vocat.**   Gaius calls the girl.
> **puella Gaium vocat.**   The girl calls Gaius.

In the first case, **"Gaius"** is the **subject** and **"the girl"** the **object** – so the ending of **puella** changes to **puellam**. In the second **"the girl"** is the **subject** and **"Gaius"** the **object** – so the ending of **Gaius** changes to **Gaium**.

Nouns which end in **-a** have an object ending in **-am**.
Nouns which end in **-us** have an object ending in **-um**.

So   **puella** becomes **puellam**
     filius becomes **filium**

And note too that **puer** becomes **puerum**.

Note also that the word order in Latin is different from English:
in Latin the verb normally comes at the end of its sentence.

Before translating the following exercises note and then learn
the following nouns:

agricola	farmer
casa	house
femina	woman
cibus	food
servus	slave

And the following verbs:

amat	loves, likes
oppugnat	attacks
parat	prepares
portat	carries
spectat	watches, looks at

Remember that these, like all verbs, can always mean "is
preparing" etc. – if that sounds better.

*(If no special instruction is given before each exercise, translate Latin
sentences into English and English sentences into Latin.)*

EXERCISE 6.1

1.   puer puellam spectat.
2.   puella puerum vocat.
3.   agricola aquam portat.
4.   agricola cibum parat.
5.   Gaius Iuliam amat.

6.   femina puerum et puellam spectat.
7.   agricola casam aedificat.
8.   puella servum oppugnat.
9.   pater vinum amat.
10. Publius agricolam non spectat, sed Tulliam vocat.

EXERCISE 6.2

1.   Marcus is preparing the food.
2.   The slave is carrying the water.
3.   The woman calls the farmer.
4.   The farmer does not like the slave.
5.   Gaius is watching the boy and the girl.

Now learn these verbs:

delet	destroys
movet	moves
sedet	sits
terret	frightens
videt	sees

Note too that Latin does not always use a word for "his" or "her", if the meaning is obvious:

So **pater filium amat.**
is best translated as The father loves his son.

and **Marcus amicum videt.**
Marcus sees his friend.

EXERCISE 6.3

(Take care to use either "the" or "his/her" according to what makes most sense.)

1.   mater filiam amat.
2.   pater filium terret.
3.   agricola servum videt.
4.   servus cibum movet.
5.   femina agricolam non terret.

6. Gaius amicum vocat.
7. Caesar murum oppugnat et delet.
8. puella non sedet, sed ambulat.
9. servus vinum non portat, sed sedet.
10. mater filium et filiam spectat.

EXERCISE 6.4

1. The farmer destroys the wall.
2. The slave does not see the girl.
3. The boy is moving the food.
4. The woman frightens the boy.
5. The father calls (his)* slave.

* You do not need to translate "his" – see note at the start of Exercise 6.3

Remember what was said in the previous chapter about Latin not always using words for "he" or "she", and take care when translating into English:

e.g. **pater Gaium videt. puerum vocat.**
The father sees Gaius. He calls the boy.

There is no Latin word here for "he", but we know from the ending that **puer<u>um</u>** is the **object**, not the **subject**, and so the **subject** of **vocat** must be the same as the **subject** of the previous sentence.

Occasionally we find something similar in English – you may have a school report which reads something like this:

"Michael has not always paid full attention; must try harder."

It would be better English to write "he must try harder" but we can work out that the person who must try is the same as the subject of the first part of the sentence, i.e. Michael.

EXERCISE 6.5

1. pater laborat. filiam non videt.
2. Iulia natat. Marcum vocat.
3. servus non sedet. vinum portat.
4. agricola casam spectat. sedet, non ambulat.
5. Gaius non laborat. puellam spectat.

EXERCISE 6.6

Study the picture below, and in Latin write three short sentences to describe what is happening in it.

EXERCISE 6.7

1. Explain the meaning of the following English words, and show how they derive from Latin:

   agriculture   delete   preparation   terror

2. Find English derivatives from the following Latin words, and write a sentence for each to show its meaning clearly:

   femina   portat   spectat   video

ROMAN HOUSES

In this chapter you were introduced to the word **casa**, meaning "a house". This word usually described only a rather modest house, often in the country, and yet this is the word which has survived into modern Italian and Spanish as the regular word for "a house".

In towns, better-off families lived in a **domus.** Some of these would, of course, be bigger and better furnished than others. Usually they faced on to the street, with one or two small windows at the front. There would be no front garden, as is usual today, but there was a courtyard at the back, enclosed within the walls of the house to give greater privacy. This was called the **peristylium**. The garden itself was the **hortus.**

The main room of a **domus** was the **atrium** – a word now popular again to describe large areas in hotels, shops etc. This room was originally the centre of family life, where the fireplace or hearth stood, and the word **atrium** comes from a word meaning "black" – because of the black soot and smoke! However, as houses became larger and grander, so did the **atrium,** and it was used to entertain visitors.

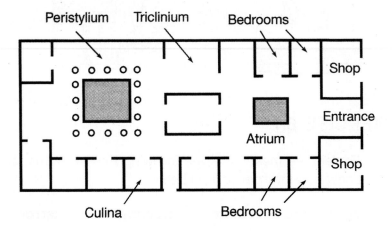

Above is the plan of a large **domus** from Pompeii, the city destroyed by the volcano Vesuvius in AD 79. You will also see other rooms marked, like the **triclinium** (dining-room) and **culina** (kitchen).

However, many of the less well-off lived in flats. We call these "blocks", but the Romans called them **insulae** (islands). These might often include shops, and small houses as well. Sometimes these were five storeys high, and might contain several small, uncomfortable rooms. It could also be risky to live here, as the **insulae** were dangerous fire hazards. They were also not always well-built, and might fall down!

Finally, in the country a rich family would live in a **villa.** If they were very wealthy they might have a **domus** in town and a **villa** in the country as well – just like some people today. A villa, however, was more than just a large country-house; it was also often a working farm and would house many slaves to do the work. In some of the villas which have been excavated there is evidence of an underground heating system **(hypocaustum)**, which enabled several rooms to be heated at once – just as modern central heating systems do. So you can see that many wealthy Romans were able to live in considerable comfort – much more so in fact than, say, the barons of the Middle Ages in their draughty castles!

EXERCISE 6.8

1. Draw a plan of your own house, and compare it with that of a Roman **domus.** In what ways are they similar or different?

2. Reread the passage above, and then explain the following Latin terms:

    a) **atrium**
    b) **triclinium**
    c) **peristylium**
    d) **villa**
    e) **hypocaustum**

In AD 79, Mount Vesuvius erupted, burying the town of Pompeii under a mass of ash. Picture courtesy of David Camden.

SINGULAR AND PLURAL

7

In the last chapter everything we met was in the **singular,** describing just one boy, one girl or whatever.

Now consider the following sentence:

> **Gaius puell<u>as</u> vocat.**
> Gaius calls the girl<u>s</u>.

Latin – like English – changes the ending to show that it is more than one girl being called. This is called a **plural** ending.

Now look carefully at this sentence:

> **puell<u>ae</u> Gaium voca<u>nt</u>.**
> The girl<u>s</u> call Gaius.

Here two changes have been made – again just like English.

puellae is in the **plural,** showing that there is more than one girl doing the calling.

vocant is also in the **plural** because it means "<u>they call</u>" rather than "she calls".

All verbs end in **-t** when they mean "he, she or it" does something and in **-nt** when they mean "they" do something.

You must learn these two verb endings, and now learn the noun endings as well.

You should now learn that the **subject** and **object** endings are known as **cases.**

The **subject** is the **nominative case,** and the **object** is the **accusative case.**

	SINGULAR	PLURAL
NOMINATIVE	puella	puellae
ACCUSATIVE	puellam	puellās
NOMINATIVE	servus	servi
ACCUSATIVE	servum	servōs

Before translating the exercises in this chapter note and learn the following new nouns:

Like puella:

dea	goddess
fabula	story
mensa	table

Like servus:

deus	god

And the following verbs:

curat	looks after
intrat	enters
narrat	tells
habet	has
monet	warns, advises
timet	fears

EXERCISE 7.1

1. dea puellas curat.
2. Gaius tres fabulas narrat.
3. servi non laborant.
4. feminae villam intrant.
5. puer amicos vocat.
6. agricola quattuor filias habet.
7. deus servos terret.
8. deae puerum monent.
9. Iulia pueros non timet.
10. decem servi mensas movent.

EXERCISE 7.2

1. agricolae muros delent.
2. pueri puellas vocant.
3. pater filios monet.
4. Caesar pueros et puellas terret.
5. pueri ambulant, sed puellae festinant.
6. mater filios et filias amat.
7. servi luliam vident et timent.
8. quinque feminae aquam et cibum portant.
9. agricolae atrium non intrant.
10. deae hortum spectant. pueros vident.

EXERCISE 7.3

Write the following in the plural and then translate.

1. agricola deum vocat.
2. servus mensam movet.
3. puella fabulam narrat.
4. puer amicum non videt.
5. femina casam intrat.

EXERCISE 7.4

1. The girls are swimming.
2. The boys are not working.
3. The farmers do not see the food.
4. The slave does not fear the boys.
5. The woman is telling stories.
6. Gaius sees the girls.
7. The god and the goddess are approaching.
8. The farmers attack the villa.
9. Nine slaves are carrying the tables.
10. The father frightens (his) sons.

EXERCISE 7.5

Write three Latin sentences to describe what is happening in the picture below.

EXERCISE 7.6

1. Explain the meaning of the following English words, and show how they derive from Latin:

    deify   fabulous   sediment   servile

2. Find English derivatives from the following Latin words, and write a sentence for each to show its meaning clearly:

    curat   monet   narrat   timet

ROMAN GODS

In this chapter you have met the Latin words for "god" and "goddess" – **deus** and **dea.** The Romans did not have just one God, as so many world religions have today, but they believed in many different gods.

To begin with, the earliest Romans believed that there was a spirit in every natural thing around them. The early farmers, who depended on nature for the success of their crops and therefore their livelihood, imagined that there were spirits in their fields and their crops, and also in the weather, the rivers, woods, fountains and springs. For this reason they would often make offerings of wine and food, or even do something which we would find offensive – sacrifice an animal.

After a while these early Romans came into contact with the **Greeks** who had settled in southern Italy. These Greeks brought with them their own ideas about religion and built temples to their gods and goddesses, who they believed lived on top of a great mountain called **Olympus** in Greece. These gods and goddesses were thought to be all-powerful, and there were many stories and legends told about them.

Here is a list of these great gods and goddesses – some of whom you have probably already heard about.

Roman name	Greek name	
Jupiter	Zeus	King of gods and men; god of weather
Juno	Hera	Wife of Jupiter; goddess of marriage
Apollo	Apollo	God of enlightenment, prophecy and music
Diana	Artemis	Goddess of the moon and hunting
Neptune	Poseidon	God of the sea and earthquakes
Minerva	Athene	Goddess of wisdom and crafts
Mars	Ares	God of war
Venus	Aphrodite	Goddess of love and beauty
Vulcan	Hephaestus	God of fire and metalworking
Ceres	Demeter	Goddess of crops
Bacchus	Dionysus	God of wine, partying and drama
Mercury	Hermes	Messenger of the gods

EXERCISE 7.7

1. In what other ways are the names of some of these gods and goddesses used today? For instance, where else have you heard of Mars or Apollo in a modern context?

2. Find out more about some of the gods and goddesses in the list above. Try to find a story about one of them which you consider especially interesting and exciting and tell it to the rest of the class.

3. Why did the early Romans believe so much in the world around them? Do you think they were wrong to make sacrifices of young animals to the spirits of the countryside?

4. Why do you think that the Greeks and the Romans believed in so many gods and goddesses?

5. Here is a picture of a statue of Zeus from the National Archaeological Museum in Athens shown hurling a thunderbolt — though some people believe that it is Poseidon hurling his trident. What do you think?

6.   Draw a picture of another god or goddess, showing, if possible, their area of special power.

According to Greek and Roman myth, the world and all the heavens were carried on the shoulders of a Titan called Atlas, pictured here. Picture courtesy of David Camden; statue in the National Archaeological Museum in Naples (Italy).

VERB TABLES

8

In the previous chapters we have met verbs when the subject of the verb has always been "he", "she" or "they". These are known as the **3rd person**; we shall now look at the other persons:

1st person is **I** and **we**
2nd person is **you**

In Latin the normal order for learning a verb is as follows:

1st person singular	**I**
2nd person singular	**You** (talking to one person)
3rd person singular	**He, she, it**
1st person plural	**We**
2nd person plural	**You** (talking to more than one person)
3rd person plural	**They**

There are endings in Latin which show each of these as follows:

-o	**I**
-s	**You** (singular)
-t	**He, she, it**
-mus	**We**
-tis	**You** (plural)
-nt	**They**

Once you have learnt these endings, you should be able to work out what every verb means, e.g.

ambul**o**	**I** walk
clam**amus**	**We** shout
vid**etis**	**You** see

EXERCISE 8.1

1. intramus
2. monetis
3. habeo
4. vocatis
5. narras
6. moveo
7. natant
8. sedet
9. porto
10. amamus

In Latin there are four different types of verbs, and the verbs so far used belong to the first two types.

The first type has an **-a-** before the endings and the second has an **-e-**. Note how the **-a-** disappears before the **-o** in the 1st person singular.

amo	I love; I am loving
amās	You love; you are loving
amat	He, she, it loves; he, she, it is loving
amāmus	We love; we are loving
amātis	You love; you are loving
amant	They love; they are loving

video	I see; I am seeing
vidēs	You see; you are seeing
videt	He, she, it sees; he, she, it is seeing
vidēmus	We see; we are seeing
vidētis	You see; you are seeing
vident	They see; they are seeing

All the verbs you have so far learnt ending in **-at** belong to the first type, and all those ending in **-et** belong to the second.

Learn the above tables before translating the next exercises.

EXERCISE 8.2

1. aedificas.
2. cantamus.
3. appropinquo.
4. terremus.
5. sedes.
6. paro.
7. festinamus.
8. ambulas.
9. movetis.
10. habet.

EXERCISE 8.3

1. We warn.
2. They build.
3. I have.
4. You (s) are destroying.
5. You (pl) are walking.
6. They look after.
7. She is calling.
8. We are swimming.
9. I enter.
10. They attack.

EXERCISE 8.4

1. hortum intramus.
2. filiam moneo.
3. puellas amamus.
4. fabulam narras.
5. cibum porto.
6. aquam non habent.
7. murum aedificatis.
8. servos spectat.
9. agricolam curamus.
10. mensas movent.

EXERCISE 8.5

(When translating "you" into Latin, you can decide whether to make it singular or plural.)

1. I am telling a story.
2. You are looking after the girls.
3. We see the farmer.
4. They are destroying the tables.
5. I do not have a son.
6. You are carrying the food and water.
7. We are warning the slaves.
8. She is preparing the food.
9. You frighten the women.
10. We watch the farmers.

Here are some new verbs to note and then learn:

Like **amo:**

exspecto	I wait for
iuvo	I help
saluto	I greet

Like **video:**

doceo	I teach
teneo	I hold
timeo	I fear, am afraid (of)

EXERCISE 8.6

1. puellas exspectamus.
2. pueros doceo.
3. navigatis et timetis.
4. mensam teneo.
5. filiam iuvo.
6. agricolam non timemus.
7. amicos iuvamus.
8. cibum exspectatis.
9. Minervam timent.
10. Bacchum salutant.

EXERCISE 8.7

1. I am helping the farmer.
2. We are watching the girls.
3. They greet Gaius.
4. We are waiting for the slaves.
5. He teaches boys and girls.

In Chapters 5 and 6 we saw how **clamat** can mean just "shouts" or "he shouts" – this is because it is not necessary to include a subject pronoun like "he" in Latin as all the verb endings in Latin are different.

So we can tell from the ending that **clamo** means "I shout" rather than "they shout" or "we shout".

But there are words in Latin for "I", "you" etc. and these are often used, especially if we need to emphasise exactly who is doing something.

So   **ego sto, vos sedetis**

means   **I** am standing, (but) **you** are sitting.

The words for "I" and "you" are used here to give the emphasis.

Now look at the verb **amo** with the pronouns and see how closely it compares with French.

ego amo	j'aime	I love
tu amas	tu aimes	you love
ille amat	il aime	he loves
illa amat	elle aime	she loves
nos amamus	nous aimons	we love
vos amatis	vous aimez	you love
illi amant	ils aiment	they (masculine) love
illae amant	elles aiment	they (feminine) love

Latin will quite often use these pronouns to provide emphasis or contrast, but they are usually left out.

So	**ego casam video**
and	**casam video**
both mean	I see the house

ille, illa, illi and **illae** are often used to highlight the person/people just mentioned.

e.g.	**Marcum spectamus. ille pugnat.**
	We are watching Marcus. He is fighting.

EXERCISE 8.8

1. ego agricolam timeo.
2. nos puellas videmus.
3. illi fabulam narrant.
4. ego aquam porto, tu cibum tenes.
5. ego ambulo, vos navigatis.
6. Gaium video. ille natat.
7. servos spectamus. illi vinum portant.
8. mater puellam vocat. illa non iuvat.
9. ego te exspecto, sed tu non appropinquas.
10. ego pueros doceo. illi laborant.

EXERCISE 8.9

(Use pronouns only if you wish to emphasise the "I" etc.)

1. I am preparing the food.
2. We are building a house.
3. You are helping (your)* friends.
4. I am hurrying, you are sitting.
5. We greet the boys. They are approaching.

* There is no need to translate "your" (just like "his/her" – see note on p.43)

RELIGION IN THE HOME

In the last chapter we looked at the major **Olympian gods and goddesses** who would be publicly worshipped on special festival days. However, religion also played an important part in the everyday life of a Roman family at home.

You read in the last chapter how the early Romans thought that there were spirits all around them. This applied to their homes as well, and you read in Chapter 6 about different types of Roman houses. However large or small his home was, the owner believed that the gods looked after it and that these gods needed to be kept happy so that the family would be protected by them.

These family gods were called **lares** and **penates**. The **lares** were thought to be spirits of the family's ancestors, and in the **atrium** (see Chapter 6) there was a shrine called the **lararium** where these would be worshipped.

The **penates** were thought to be the spirits who protected the family's store cupboard, and it was, of course, important to keep these gods happy so that the family had enough to eat!

You will, I hope, remember that the **atrium** took its name from the fireplace or hearth which originally stood at the centre of that room. The hearth was extremely important to ordinary Romans as a means of warmth, light and cooking. They therefore worshipped the goddess of the hearth, and called her **Vesta**.

Another spirit that the Romans personalised was that of the doorway. The Latin for door is **ianua**, and the god was called **Janus**, a two-faced god who watched the doorway from both directions. The name of the month **January** comes from this, as it is the doorway of the New Year.

It was very important for the father of the family (the **paterfamilias**) to ensure that he said the prayers correctly to all these household gods and that he performed the proper rituals in the right way. Otherwise, or so they believed, the family might suffer harm. The Romans' attitude to prayer and sacrifice was very much one of hoping that by helping the gods they in turn would also be helped.

EXERCISE 8.10

1.   Revise the list of gods and goddesses on p.57 and answer the following questions:

  a) Who was the Roman god of war?

  b) Who was the Roman equivalent of Hera?

  c) What was Neptune god of?

  d) Who was the Greek god of wine?

  e) Who was the Roman goddess of the moon?

2.   Why was it important, do you think, for the Romans to worship the gods of the household?

3.   Are there any modern religious customs which you think are in any way similar to the way the Romans worshipped their gods?

Slavery was a simple fact of life in the Roman Empire. Rich households owned many slaves, and could treat them as they wished. Some slaves were treated like family members, others like possessions.

POSSESSION

9

Consider the following sentences:

> There is **Michael's** book
> Where is the **boy's** sister?
> What is the name **of the river**?

In each of these three examples, the words in bold show **possession**. The book belongs to Michael, the sister to the boy and the name to the river.

In English we either express this by using the word **of** or by using the ending **-'s**.

In Latin **possession** is shown only by an ending, and this is known as the **genitive case**.

The **genitive** endings for nouns like **puella** are:
    -ae in the singular and **-ārum** in the plural

and for nouns like servus:
    -ī in the singular and **-ōrum** in the plural

So   **filius SERVI**
means   The son OF THE SLAVE
or   The SLAVE'S son

and can be written in reverse order (rather like the English):

SERVI filius

and   **fabulae AGRICOLARUM**
or   **AGRICOLARUM fabulae**
both mean   The stories OF THE FARMERS
or   THE FARMERS' stories

EXERCISE 9.1

1.   filius agricolae non laborat.
2.   Gaius filiam Iuliae vocat.
3.   casam puellarum videmus.
4.   servi cibum feminarum portant.
5.   ianuam casae spectamus.
6.   servi agricolae ambulant, non festinant.
7.   muros agricolarum delemus.
8.   filia deae fabulam narrat.
9.   amicus agricolae puellas spectat.
10. Minerva filios Iuliae monet.

EXERCISE 9.2

1.   Julia's slaves are not working.
2.   I help the farmer's daughter.
3.   We are moving the woman's tables.
4.   I am watching the houses of (my) friends.
5.   Six slaves are carrying the girls' water.

Note and then learn these new nouns before doing the next exercises.

Like **puella**:

incola	inhabitant
ira	anger
nauta	sailor
pecunia	money
poeta	poet
regina	queen

Like **servus**:

equus	horse
gladius	sword
nuntius	messenger, message

EXERCISE 9.3

1. Bacchus incolas insulae terret.
2. incolae iram dei timent.
3. pecuniam puerorum habeo.
4. nos equos reginae spectamus.
5. reginae nuntius festinat.
6. nautae filium poetae oppugnant.
7. pueri fabulas poetarum amant.
8. puellae puerorum pecuniam movent.
9. servi gladios nautarum tenent.
10. equi deorum puellas terrent.

EXERCISE 9.4

1. I see the farmer's house.
2. We are preparing the queen's food.
3. We have the messenger's sword.
4. The gods are destroying the houses of the inhabitants.
5. The farmer's slaves are watching the door of the house.

EXERCISE 9.5

Write two or three Latin sentences to describe what is happening in the picture below.

SLAVES

It seems appropriate in this chapter about possession to discuss slaves. The first thing to bear in mind about slaves – who formed such an integral part of life in the ancient world (in Greece and Egypt as well as Rome) – is that they were <u>owned</u> by their masters.

You have now come across the Latin word for "slave" (**servus**) many times. Even less well-off Roman citizens owned a slave or two, whereas the wealthy might have owned several hundred. Some slaves were treated reasonably well and others with appalling cruelty, and masters were able to kill their slaves, if they wished, without being punished.

Even those who treated their slaves well were often doing so, not out of kindness, but out of self-interest. Because slaves were possessions, they were probably regarded as things rather than as people, and owners might look after them well in the same way that you might look after your tennis racket well – so that it doesn't wear out too quickly and you then have to buy a new one!

Very few people (if any!) in our society would regard slavery as anything other than dreadful, but it was accepted as normal by the Romans. There would be slaves in the town and slaves in the country, and some of the worst conditions were in the mines or in the galleys – as you might have seen in the old film *Ben Hur*.

It is difficult to estimate the number of slaves, but it was certainly a very high proportion of the total population. It is therefore surprising that the slaves did not often turn against their masters. There was one very famous uprising during the lifetime of Julius Caesar, led by a man called **Spartacus** (again this was made into a film). He managed to defeat several Roman armies and ravage much of Italy with his huge band of slaves before he was finally defeated.

Never again do we hear of an uprising on this scale. However, there were other smaller incidents recorded such as this successful attempt on a master's life which happened in the first century AD:

"Larcius Macedo suffered a terrible fate at the hands of his own slaves. He was washing in his villa, when suddenly his slaves surrounded him. One took him by the throat, another punched him in the face, another hit his stomach! When they thought him dead, they threw him on to a hot floor to check whether he was in fact still breathing. Macedo, fearing death, lay as still as possible, and was then overcome by the heat. He was carried out from the hot room, and loyal slaves came rushing to see what had happened. The cool of the air revived him, and he opened his eyes, thus showing that he was alive. The guilty slaves fled, and most of them were soon arrested and executed. The loyal slaves nursed Macedo for a few days, but he then died – with the satisfaction of having seen his murder avenged."

It has to be said that some slaves did in the end lead a good life. If slaves were paid a little money, they could save it and then buy their freedom, and in certain cases a kindly master might grant freedom to a slave. A freed slave was called a freedman (**libertus**), and, although there was an undoubted snobbery against such people, they could become very rich and sometimes powerful. The emperor **Claudius** (who reigned AD 41–54 and invaded Britain – see Chapter 11) relied heavily on freedmen, men like **Pallas** and **Narcissus**, who held great influence over him.

Unfortunately, slavery was not confined to the ancient world. In later centuries, the British played an active and shameful part in the slave trade across the Atlantic, until it was abolished here in the early 19th century.

Even today we read of children being used as slave labour in many parts of what is known as the Third World, i.e. the poorer countries of Africa, Asia and South America. And there have been cases in many countries of maids being used as slaves in rich people's homes.

EXERCISE 9.6

1. Try to find out more about slavery in the Roman world. Find out how they were bought and sold, and what happened to them if they tried to run away.

2. Try to find out about more recent slavery, for example, in the USA. Why do you think people used slaves in this way?

3. Do you agree that slavery is cruel? If so, why do you think that it lasted for so long?

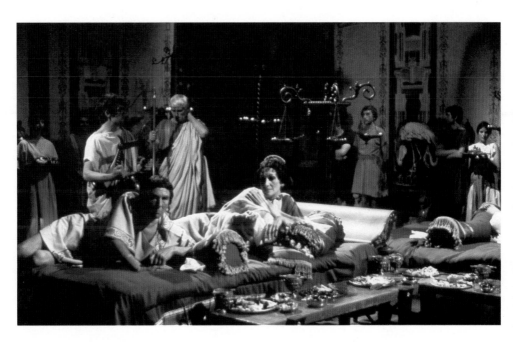

*Romans usually ate their meals around the **triclinium**, as seen above in a scene from the series 'I Claudius'. Daytime meals were often small, but the evening **cena** could be a great feast with a variety of foods and wine. Picture courtesy of the BBC.*

INDIRECT OBJECT

10

Consider the following sentences:

> I give <u>the book</u> **to the boy.**
> We show <u>the way</u> **to the strangers**.
> I am cooking <u>a meal</u> **for my family.**

In each of these sentences the words underlined are the object which we discussed in Chapter 6. This is sometimes called the direct object.

The words in bold are a second object of the verb, which we call the **indirect object**, often introduced in English by the words "to" or "for", but not always – as you can see from another way of expressing these three sentences:

> I give **the boy** <u>the book</u>.
> We show **the strangers** <u>the way</u>.
> I am cooking **my family** <u>a meal</u>.

Note how here the **indirect object** has no word in front of it, but always comes before the direct object.

You know that in Latin the direct object goes into the accusative case. The **indirect object** is shown by another case ending. This is known as the **dative case** – the "giving" case from the verb **do** meaning "I give" which you will shortly meet.

The **dative** endings for nouns like puella are:
> **-ae** in the singular and **-īs** in the plural

and for nouns like servus:
> **-ō** in the singular and **-īs** in the plural

So   **Gaius cibum SERVO dat**

Means   Gaius gives food TO THE SLAVE

or   Gaius gives THE SLAVE food

When translating into English choose the way which seems more natural, and note that in Latin too the word order can vary, putting the **indirect object** before the direct object.

So   **mater PUELLIS pecuniam dat**

means   The mother gives THE GIRLS money

or   The mother gives money TO THE GIRLS

These new verbs should be learnt before translating the next exercises.

Like amo:

        do   I give

        monstro   I show, point out

Like video:

        respondeo   I reply

EXERCISE 10.1

1. pater equum filio dat.
2. servus cibum Gaio parat.
3. puellis fabulam narro.
4. pecuniam incolis insulae damus.
5. Iulia amicis ianuam monstrat.
6. femina agricolae non respondet.
7. puellae cibum et aquam poetae dant.
8. pueri reginae respondent.
9. servi mensas agricolis parant.
10. Claudius libertis pecuniam dat.

EXERCISE 10.2

1. I am giving money to the farmers.
2. The boy is pointing out the island to the sailors.
3. We are preparing food for Tullia.
4. The girls do not reply to the boys.
5. The poet is telling the boys a story.

Learn these new nouns before doing the next exercises.

Like **puella:**

cena	dinner
epistola	letter
hasta	spear
sagitta	arrow
via	road, way

Like **servus:**

taurus	bull
ventus	wind

EXERCISE 10.3

1. Tullia Marco epistolam monstrat.
2. Publius cibum servis dat.
3. servi cenam Publio parant.
4. nautae hastas et sagittas reginae monstrant.
5. taurum agricolae damus.
6. deus ventum nautis dat.
7. Minerva viam servo monstrat.
8. nuntii tres epistolas Claudio dant.
9. Gaius Iuliam vocat. illa puero non respondet.
10. servi mensas portant. cenam Iuliae parant.

EXERCISE 10.4

1. We show the letter to the freedman.
2. The goddess gives the sailor a wind.
3. Five girls are preparing dinner for Publius.
4. The boys do not reply to the poet.
5. The sailors are giving swords and spears to the slaves.

EXERCISE 10.5

Write three Latin sentences to describe what is happening in the picture below.

EXERCISE 10.6

1. Explain the meaning of the following English words, and show how they derive from Latin:

    indoctrinate   equestrian   salutation   viaduct

2. Find English derivatives from the following Latin words, and write a sentence for each to show its meaning clearly:

    epistola   monstrat   nauta   respondet

3. What do the following signs of the Zodiac mean?

    Aquarius   Taurus   Sagittarius

FOOD AND DRINK

You have now met the word **cena** meaning "dinner". Therefore, this seems a good time to learn more about Roman meals.

The **cena** was the main meal of the day: it began around what we would consider to be teatime and often lasted for more than three hours. This was partly because the Romans would have eaten little prior to this main meal: they might snatch a bite of breakfast (**ientaculum**) before going off to work, and then a light lunch (**prandium**) around noon when they stopped work. This **prandium** was usually cold leftovers from the previous night's **cena**.

*A reconstruction of a Roman **culina**, courtesy of L. Noles*

Poorer families – just as today – ate less food than the rich, often little more than bread, olives, perhaps occasionally a little meat, some honey to sweeten things and rough wine to wash it all down. The wealthy, however, could be very self-indulgent and there was little of the concern for healthy eating which has developed in our country in recent years. The **cena** consisted of three courses, but each of these often contained several separate dishes. These courses were as follows:

gustatio	hors d'oeuvres
primae mensae	meat, fish or poultry
secundae mensae	dessert

We are fortunate to have a Roman cookery book, written by a man called **Apicius**. He gives a wide variety of recipes, suitable for both rich and poor families. Some of these you could try yourselves, but you might wish to avoid the more exotic dishes like sow's udders, sea-urchins or dormice stuffed with pine kernels

The rich drank good wine and plenty of it, but Roman wine was usually mixed with water to dilute it. If people were entertaining guests, they would often employ singers and even acrobats to amuse the party. Some more extravagant dinner-parties went on for much of the night. The idea of Roman orgies may be an exaggeration, but the Romans did know how to enjoy themselves!

The **cena** took place in the **triclinium** (see Chapter 6). This name for a dining-room came from the three couches (**lecti**) that were placed round for the diners to recline on. Slaves cut up the food in advance so that it could be more easily eaten by hand.

EXERCISE 10.7

1. Make a list of what your family normally eats for breakfast, lunch and dinner. How different do you think this is from what the Romans ate?

2. Imagine that you are opening a restaurant in ancient Rome. Draw a poster to advertise it.

3. See if you can borrow a copy of Apicius' Cookbook (perhaps from your local library) and attempt some of the dishes.

Roman battle of the sort that would have occurred between the inhabitants of Scotland and the Roman army defending Hadrian's wall. Picture courtesy of Ronald Embleton.

PREPOSITIONS 11

In English there are certain little words which introduce a new noun into the sentence and describe its location or situation. These are words like "in", "at", "under" etc. and they are called **prepositions.**

e.g.

in the study   on a chair

at a desk   before supper

under the tree   after tennis

In Latin, as in English, there are various prepositions, but in Latin prepositions have an effect on the ending of the noun.

Several prepositions are followed by the **accusative case**; this is the **object** case which we met in Chapters 6 and 7. Such prepositions are:

ad	to, towards
in	into
contra	against
per	through
prope	near

So **Gaius in casam ambulat**

means Gaius is walking into the house

and **ad oram festinamus**

means We are hurrying to the shore

Note carefully the difference in English between this **to** which means "towards" and is used with verbs of **going** etc., and the **to** we met in the last chapter which is used with verbs of **giving**. In Latin this becomes the **dative case <u>without any preposition</u>**.

Before doing the next exercises learn the meanings of the prepositions above, and also of the following new nouns:

Like **puella**:

ora	shore
ripa	river-bank
silva	wood

Like **servus**:

ludus	school

EXERCISE 11.1

1. nautae ad insulam navigant.
2. pueri ad ludum non festinant.
3. septem tauri in agris errant.
4. servi tres lectos in triclinium portant.
5. Gaius et Iulia in hortum ambulant.
6. ad ianuam villae festino.
7. mater per silvam errat.
8. pueri prope ludum stant.
9. ad muros festinamus.
10. Claudius contra incolas insulae pugnat.

EXERCISE 11.2

1. The girl is walking into the garden.
2. Two boys are wandering through the woods.
3. We are standing near the walls.
4. The farmer's daughter is hurrying to the river-bank.
5. The slaves are showing the food to the girls.

There are other prepositions which take a new case which you have not yet learnt; this is called the **ablative**.

The **ablative** endings for nouns like puella are:

>   -**ā** in the singular and -**īs** in the plural

and for nouns like servus:

>   -**ō** in the singular and -**īs** in the plural

Prepositions which take the **ablative** include:

a, ab	from
e, ex	out of
cum	(together) with
in	in, on

Note that **ab** and **ex** are used before nouns beginning with a vowel or h:

So   **ab ora**   from the shore
          ex horto   out of the garden

Note too that **in** with the **accusative** means **into** or **on to**, but **in** with the **ablative** means **in** or **on**

So   **IN HORTUM ambulo**
       I walk **INTO THE GARDEN**

       IN HORTO sedeo
       I am sitting **IN THE GARDEN**

EXERCISE 11.3

1. servi e culina ambulant.
2. cibum in hortum portant.
3. Gaius in horto cum Iulia cibum exspectat.
4. Gaius et Iulia ad ripam errant.
5. Iulia servos prope casam videt.
6. mater cum filia in horto sedet.
7. femina fabulam filiae narrat.
8. puella ex horto ad silvas errat.
9. mater per silvas ambulat et filiam videt.
10. libertus servos in casam vocat. illi ex horto festinant.

EXERCISE 11.4

1. We are sitting in the garden.
2. The girls are hurrying from the river-bank.
3. Gaius is sitting with Julia.
4. Mother is walking into the garden with Marcus.
5. The slaves are moving eight tables out of the kitchen.

EXERCISE 11.5

Write two Latin sentences to describe what is happening in the picture below.

ROMAN BRITAIN

You read in chapters 1 and 2 a little about the might of the **Roman Empire**. If you look again at the map on p.4, you can see how far Rome's empire stretched. The most northerly province of the Empire was our own country of **Great Britain**, where Roman influence lasted for nearly five hundred years.

Julius Caesar was the first Roman to invade Britain, although he did not actually conquer it. He led two expeditions in **55** BC and one in **54** BC.

Even though he did not bring Britain under direct Roman rule, he won enormous prestige from having visited such a far-flung land, and from having successfully led an army there and back again.

Caesar did establish treaties with some of the rulers living in south-east Britain, and over the next hundred years Roman traders visited Britain frequently. The kings and aristocrats of the south-east began to buy Roman goods, such as wine and olive oil, and thus to adopt Roman habits. Some kings even used Latin on their coins, like the one below where you can clearly see the Latin word for king: **rex**. We also know of at least one who advertised his "Roman-ness" by putting a vine leaf on his coins.

It was almost exactly one hundred years after Caesar's expeditions that the emperor **Claudius** led a full-scale invasion of the country. He sent a commander ahead, and then he himself arrived (with a band of elephants to impress the enemy!) and secured **Britannia** as a new province of the Roman empire.

In spite of the initial victories, some British leaders were unhappy about Roman rule, and one of them, **Caratacus**, escaped to Wales. He led a guerrilla campaign for a few years until he was at last defeated. He escaped after the battle, but was then betrayed by another British ruler. However, when he was taken to Rome, he was pardoned by Claudius and allowed to live there in some comfort.

There were other troubles, such as **Boudicca's Revolt** (which you will read about in the next chapter), but otherwise the Roman occupation of Britain was remarkably peaceful. **Towns** and **roads** were built in the Roman style, and many of the inhabitants enjoyed the peace and prosperity that Roman rule brought. This is often known as **Pax Romana** (Roman peace). Several Britons became very wealthy, living in large **villas**, just like Roman citizens in any other part of the Empire.

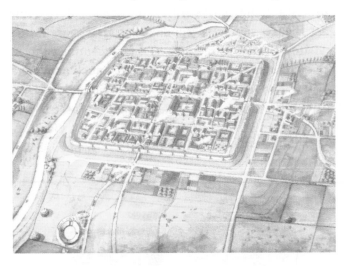

A reconstruction of a Roman town seen from above. Picture by Susan White.

In the third century AD, when other parts of the Empire began to suffer from raids by marauding tribes, Britain remained peaceful. However, Britain too came to be attacked by other peoples such as the Saxons, and soon after AD 400 the Romans were unable to pour in further troops to defend Britain, because of troubles nearer to home. Roman influence did continue for a while, but by AD 500 it had largely disappeared under the harsh rule of the Saxons.

EXERCISE 11.6

1. In what ways do you think that Britain benefited from several centuries of Roman rule? Do you think that any of these benefits have survived until today?

2. Imagine that you are a travel agent in Ancient Rome. Devise a poster to attract your customers to visit Britain for a holiday.

Boudicca, known by the Romans as Boadicea, was the queen of one of the bigger tribes in Britain, the Iceni. After being deeply insulted by the invading Romans, she led a large army of Britons against the occupying army. After some initial success, her army was eventually beaten, and as a result she killed herself. Picture courtesy of Mark Hegarty.

SIMPLE QUESTIONS

12

There are several simple question words in Latin, just as there are in English, and the following should now be learnt:

cur?	why?
ubi?	where?
quis?	who?
quid?	what?
quot?	how many?

EXERCISE 12.1

1. cur ad ludum festinas?
2. quis in horto sedet?
3. quot nautae ad insulam navigant?
4. quid puellae vident?
5. ubi pueri stant?
6. cur libertus ex horto ambulat?
7. cur agricola murum aedificat?
8. quis filiam agricolae oppugnat?
9. quid in via videtis?
10. quot mensas portatis?

EXERCISE 12.2

1. Who is wandering into the wood?
2. Why are you walking with the girls?
3. Why are the farmers hurrying out of the house?
4. How many bulls do you have?
5. Where are you watching the queen's horses?

EXERCISE 12.3

Look at the following pictures, and answer the questions below in Latin.

1. ubi sedet puella?

2. quid servi portant?

3. quot servi in horto laborant?

4. quis in via ambulat?

If there is no actual question word like "who?" "why?" etc., then Latin simply attaches the letters -**ne** to the end of the first word to show that it is a question.

> **festinasne?**
> Are you hurrying?

> **puerine in ludum ambulant?**
> Are the children walking to school?

NB: *'pueri'* (*in the plural*) *can mean 'boys' or 'children' (i.e. boys <u>and</u> girls)*

EXERCISE 12.4

1. videsne puellam?
2. aquamne habemus?
3. monstrasne viam agricolis?
4. cibumne pueris paratis?
5. ubi casam aedificas?
6. tune in hortum ambulas?
7. vosne pecuniam puellis datis?
8. cur rex feminis non respondet?
9. taurumne spectas? erratne in agro?
10. cur pueri in via stant? Iuliamne expectant?

EXERCISE 12.5

1. Are you giving the letter to the girl?
2. Are you sailing towards the island?
3. Are the boys looking after the spears?
4. Do the slaves fear the farmer?
5. Do you see Tullia? Is she sitting in the garden?

If the question is negative, then Latin always begins with **non** and by adding -**ne** turns it into **nonne**?

> **nonne festinas?**
> Aren't you hurrying?

> **nonne servi laborant?**
> Aren't the slaves working?

or   Surely the slaves are working?

This type of question usually expects a "yes" answer. To ask a question expecting a "no" answer, Latin uses **num?** meaning "surely ... not?"

> **num tu agricolam times?**
> Surely you are <u>not</u> afraid of the farmer?

EXERCISE 12.6

1.   nonne cibum et aquam habetis?
2.   nonne tu taurum agricolae times?
3.   num in silvam ambulamus?
4.   num prope ripam puellae natant?
5.   festinantne nuntii?
6.   num servi in horto sedent?
7.   paterne fabulam pueris narrat?
8.   nonne tu puellas mones?
9.   cur regina agricolas vocat?
10. num Claudius Britanniam cum elephantis oppugnat?

EXERCISE 12.7

1.   Surely you see the shore?
2.   Surely you are not fighting?
3.   Why are you giving money to the slaves?
4.   Surely you are preparing dinner in the kitchen?
5.   Surely you are not destroying the poet's house?

BOUDICCA'S REVOLT

You may well have heard of **Boudicca**, the famous queen who led a massive rebellion against the Romans within twenty years of their conquest.

You have now come across the Latin word for queen (**regina**) several times, but the Romans were unused to women ruling, and they found it very odd that the British should allow women to rule over tribes. Boudicca became queen of a tribe called the **Iceni** who lived in what is now Norfolk. After her husband died, she was expected to take over, but the Roman emperor **Nero** had other ideas, and he sent in his troops to seize the kingdom. Boudicca and her two daughters were very badly treated, and this led the Iceni and other neighbouring tribes to revolt.

The Roman governor of the province was far away, fighting in North Wales. Boudicca – who appears to have had a very strong personality – led her furious forces against the three newly established Roman towns **Colchester, St Albans** and **London**. They completely destroyed these towns and treated the inhabitants with the utmost cruelty.

It looked to some that the new province of Britain was lost. However, Boudicca's troops consisted of simple farmers who had been stirred up by their own anger and resentment and by the fierce passion of their queen. They were therefore no match for the might of the well-disciplined Roman army. Also some tribes in other parts of the province were unwilling to join Boudicca until they were convinced that she would win.

Here is a description of Boudicca from an ancient writer:

"She was very tall and grim in appearance, with a piercing gaze and a harsh voice. She had a mass of fair hair which she grew down to her hips, and wore a gold torque and a multi-coloured tunic folded round her, over which was a thick cloak fastened with a brooch. This was how she always dressed."

This is a torque of the sort that Boudicca might have worn. This particular piece of jewellery, which is made of gold, was found in Staffordshire,

The governor had marched hastily back from Wales to meet his enemy. There was a fierce battle but Boudicca's troops were easily defeated. It is written that 80,000 British were killed compared to only 400 Romans – but this is of course a Roman historian writing, and we do have to be careful about accepting his statistics! The queen herself took poison to avoid capture by the Romans.

EXERCISE 12.8

1. From the description given above draw a picture of Queen Boudicca.
2. Why do you think that Boudicca was unable to defeat the Romans?

The Roman emperor Hadrian built a famous wall across Northern
England that has lasted for centuries. During the Roman occupation of
Britannia, the wall, which marked the northern edge of the Roman Empire,
was the scene of many small battles and ambushes. Picture courtesy of
Ronald Embleton.

ADDRESSING PEOPLE

13

You have now come across many verbs using the "you" form (the 2nd person) with or without the Latin words for "you" – **tu** and **vos** (see Chapter 8).

e.g. **cur tu deam times?**
Why are you afraid of the goddess?

If we want to mention the person we are talking to or addressing, then we put this name or noun into what is called the **vocative case.**

You will recognise that the word **vocative** means "calling" from vocat and that this is therefore "the calling case".

So **cur tu deam times, Iulia?**
means Why are you afraid of the goddess, Julia?

You will see that the vocative ending above is the same as the nominative (see Chapters 6 and 7). This is true for <u>all</u> plural endings, and <u>most</u> singular endings.

ad insulam navigatis, nautae
You are sailing to the island, sailors.

EXERCISE 13.1

1. ubi sedes, Tullia?
2. in horto sedeo, mater.
3. cur agricolam non iuvatis, pueri?
4. ad silvam ambulamus, pater.
5. quot hastas habes, nauta?

6. tres hastas habeo, Caesar.
7. cur pueros terretis, agricolae?
8. pueros non terremus, sed docemus.
9. ubi laboratis, servi?
10. in culina laboramus. cenam Marco et Iuliae paramus.

EXERCISE 13.2

1. Are you watching the house, Tullia?
2. I am walking on the river-bank, father.
3. Why are you moving the tables, slaves?
4. We are preparing dinner in the garden, Julia.
5. Boys, why are you hurrying out of school?

The only exception to the vocative ending being the same as the nominative is with nouns like **servus**. These nouns drop the **-us** and replace it with **-e**, but if the noun or name ends in **-ius**, then the **-us** is dropped altogether.

So   **cur festinas, serve?**
            Why are you hurrying, slave?

            quis appropinquat, Gai?
            Who is approaching, Gaius?

Sometimes, as in English, Latin writes an "o" before the vocative case:

            cur puellam non iuvas, o dea?
            Why don't you help the girl, O goddess?

EXERCISE 13.3

1. quis puellas monet, Gai?
2. Quintus puellas monet, pater.
3. cur per agrum ambulas, Marce?
4. tauros agricolae specto, Quinte.
5. Marce et Iulia, quot casas videtis?

6. septem casas prope oram videmus, mater.
7. Tullia, ubi sedet Gaius?
8. Gaius in triclinio cum amicis sedet.
9. nonne Boudiccam iuvatis, agricolae?
10. reginam iuvamus. Romanos oppugnamus.

EXERCISE 13.4

1. Why are you standing on the shore, Marcus?
2. I am watching the sailors, father.
3. Who is helping the farmer, Quintus?
4. Julia and Publius are working with the farmer in the fields.
5. Surely you do not fear the goddess, children?

So far when addressing people we have used either statements or – more often – questions. However, we often address somebody when we want to give them an instruction or order.

e.g.   Hurry, boys!
or   Walk to the farmer's house, Marcus.

These are commands and in Latin we need to use a new part of the verb called the **imperative** (which comes from the verb impero meaning "I command").

The **imperative** is easy to learn, for when talking to one person you use the simple verb stem and when talking to more than one person you add **-te** to the stem.

So the **imperative** of **amo** is

ama
am**ate**

and of **video**   vide
vid**ete**

And the sentences above become in Latin:

festinate, pueri
ambula ad agricolae casam, Marce.

Here are some new verbs to learn before doing the next exercises.

Like **amo**:

celo	I hide
habito	I live
laudo	I praise
servo	I keep safe

Like **video**:

maneo	I wait

EXERCISE 13.5

1. mane in culina, Quinte.
2. serva aquam, Tullia.
3. o fili, lauda Mercurium et Dianam.
4. responde reginae, Gai.
5. spectate elephantos, pueri.
6. festinate per silvas, nuntii.
7. da ventum nautis, o dea.
8. cela gladium in silvis, Marce.
9. ubi habitas, Iulia?
10. prope ludum habito, Quinte.

EXERCISE 13.6

1. Prepare food and water, boys.
2. Keep the horses safe, Marcus.
3. Women, praise the goddess Minerva.
4. Hide the money in the garden, Gaius.
5. Why are you waiting on the river-bank, Quintus?

EXERCISE 13.7

1. Explain the meaning of the following English words, and show how they derive from Latin:

    decimal   **insular**   **irate**   **vision**

2. Find English derivatives from the following Latin words, and write a sentence for each to show its meaning clearly:

    contra   **habitat**   **manet**   **quot**

HADRIAN'S WALL

After the Romans had recovered from the shock of **Boudicca's Revolt** (see Chapter 12), they then initially adopted a more peaceful approach towards the inhabitants of Britain. Instead of fighting them, the new governor encouraged building to restore the towns, destroyed by Boudicca's troops, and also to plan new towns. In this way he was hoping to show the British the benefits of Roman rule.

This policy was successful, but nevertheless within ten years or so of Boudicca's Revolt, the Romans were again pushing their frontiers forward. They soon conquered the rest of Wales and northern England, but they never managed to conquer the whole of Scotland. Several times over the centuries they tried to do so, but they did not have enough troops to keep this wild and mountainous land under control.

Instead they were content to settle on the frontier established by the emperor **Hadrian** (see Chapter 2). Hadrian was a builder rather than a conqueror, and when he visited Britain himself in AD 122, he decided that a frontier system should be built across northern England from coast to coast.

Many ancient writers declared that this system (which came to be known as **Hadrian's Wall**) was built to separate the Romans from the 'barbarians' to the north. However, although the intention may have been to cut down on petty raiding by the northern tribes, there were other important reasons for building the Wall.

The Wall was a continuous line of forts and fortlets which enabled the Romans to keep a close watch on the tribes to the north. Yet it was not built as a defensive wall against attack. It certainly enabled them to have plenty of space for their troops to rest – for whole winters, if necessary. It also allowed the Roman traders to have a base from which to spread their goods further north. This in fact helped some tribes in what is now southern Scotland to become more used to Roman ways. Finally, if Hadrian built the Wall to make a name for himself, the fact that his Wall is still famous today proves how successful he was in doing that!

So despite further attempts to bring Scotland into the Empire, again and again the Romans settled back to Hadrian's tried and tested frontier. Parts of the Wall were sometimes rebuilt, but this seems to be less because of enemy attacks than from natural decay over the years. In fact the Wall lasted very well over the centuries, but suffered more recently when around two hundred years ago people took stones from the Wall to use to encircle their own land. Yet there are many parts of the Wall which are still impressive today, and it is well worth your while to visit the forts, and to walk along the Wall itself.

EXERCISE 13.8

1. Why do you think the Romans found it so difficult to conquer Scotland?
2. Do you imagine that Roman soldiers enjoyed serving on Hadrian's Wall?

This piece of Roman art is a fresco of the centaur Chiron with his pupil Achilles. Roman schoolchildren would have learned about Greek myths and about the exploits of heroes such as Achilles, and of creatures such as the half man, half horse centaur. Picture courtesy of David Camden, exhibited at the Museo Nationale, Naples (Italy).

NOUN TABLES

14

Now that you have learnt all the case endings, you will find it useful to see them in traditional "table" form as follows:

	SINGULAR	PLURAL
NOM	puell**a**	puell**ae**
VOC	puell**a**	puell**ae**
ACC	puell**am**	puell**ās**
GEN	puell**ae**	puell**ārum**
DAT	puell**ae**	puell**īs**
ABL	puell**ā**	puell**īs**

	SINGULAR	PLURAL
NOM	serv**us**	serv**ī**
VOC	serv**e**	serv**ī**
ACC	serv**um**	serv**ōs**
GEN	serv**ī**	serv**ōrum**
DAT	serv**ō**	serv**īs**
ABL	serv**ō**	serv**īs**

There are several nouns like **servus** which have a stem in -**r** (like **puer** which you have already met). These have the same endings except for the **nominative** and **vocative** singular where there is no -**us** or -**e**. Look at the following examples.

	SINGULAR	PLURAL
N/V	puer	puerī
ACC	puer**um**	puer**ōs**
GEN	puerī	puer**ōrum**
DAT	puer**ō**	puerī s
ABL	puer**ō**	puerī s

	SINGULAR	PLURAL
N/V	ager	agrī
ACC	agr**um**	agr**ōs**
GEN	agrī	agr**ōrum**
DAT	agr**ō**	agrī s
ABL	agr**ō**	agrī s

Like **puer** are **vesper** (evening) and **vir** (man, husband)
Like **ager** (field) – i.e. dropping the **e** – are **magister** (schoolmaster) and **liber** (book).

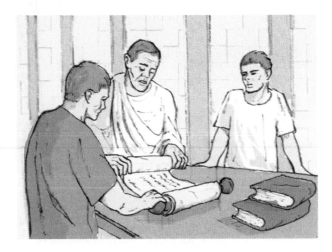

Note that there are other nouns in -er such as **pater** (father), **mater** (mother) and **frater** (brother) which you met earlier in the book. Their endings are different from those above and you will meet them at the start of the next book.

It is only worth learning case endings by rote if you clearly understand what each case ending means – if in doubt, carefully revise the previous chapters before doing the following exercises!

EXERCISE 14.1

1. magister pueros in ludo docet.
2. pueri libros in ludum portant.
3. cur in agros festinas, serve?
4. nautae ad oram insulae navigant.
5. cur hastas in agro celamus?
6. nonne cibum poetae datis, puellae?
7. viri iram deae timent.
8. magister cum poeta per hortum ambulat.
9. puer amicos prope ianuam ludi exspectat.
10. Hadrianus murum in Britannia aedificat.

EXERCISE 14.2

Rewrite the following sentences putting all nouns and verbs into the plural, and then translate into English.

1. puella servum in via videt.
2. dea virum in silva terret.
3. puer librum magistri portat.
4. nauta hastam agricolae dat.
5. cur tu in agro manes, serve?

EXERCISE 14.3

1. The schoolmaster is frightening the boys.
2. We see the farmer's bulls in the field.
3. The poet is showing the book to the girls.
4. The men do not reply to the queen.
5. Why are you moving the couches, slaves?

EXERCISE 14.4

Before translating write out the sentences in Latin, underlining each noun and saying what case it is, and whether singular or plural.

1.   magister fabulam pueris narrat.
2.   oram insulae spectamus.
3.   agricola sagittas in casa celat.
4.   cum puella per silvam ambulo.
5.   nonne taurum agricolae in agris vides, Marce?
6.   vir gladium filiae monstrat.
7.   regina incolas prope muros oppugnat.
8.   filia poetae cenam pueris in culina parat.
9.   filius magistri cum amicis in ludo manet.
10.   cur epistolam Tulliae magistro das, fili?

EXERCISE 14.5

Write two or three Latin sentences to describe what is happening in the picture below.

GOING TO SCHOOL

Going to school is something that you may or may not enjoy! It was just the same for children in the Roman world, but, as you will read, they probably had a much worse time than you do!

In this chapter you met the Latin for schoolmaster (**magister**) or, to give him his full title, **magister ludi**. Provided that his father could afford the schoolmaster's modest fee, a Roman started primary education at around six or seven, rather later than in today's world. Boys from richer families might well have a private tutor at home – just as they would have done in this country in the early 19th century. Otherwise they would go to a **ludus** to learn what are now called the three Rs: reading, writing and basic arithmetic.

The school was often just one room, perhaps next to a shop or house and sometimes open to the street. The **magister ludi** would teach all the subjects, and would have to cope with a lot of noise from the street – if not from the pupils themselves! Then, as now, schoolmasters were not well paid – it could take a schoolmaster a whole year to earn what a charioteer might earn in a single afternoon!

The poet Martial, writing around AD 100, does not paint a very rosy picture of Roman schooldays:

> "You rascally schoolmaster, hated by the girls and boys
> in your class, why do you disturb your neighbours?
> Though the cock has not yet crowed, you shatter the
> silence with your savage threats and cruel blows."

You can see from this that lessons often started very early. They would stop for a break, and then finish early in the afternoon. Children took their own books, pens and writing-tablets to school in some sort of satchel. Sometimes slaves would carry these for them. The writing-tablet (**tabula**) was made of wood covered with wax, and a pen with a sharp point

(stylus) was used to write on it. The books used were in fact scrolls, and to write on a scroll (volumen), a quill pen (penna) was used, with ink made from dye, soot or octopus-ink.

At the age of ten or eleven some children went on to secondary education. A teacher known as a **grammaticus** would teach them grammar and literature, both Latin and Greek. This stage of education is known to have been very tedious, and most certainly lacked the variety of subjects and style that exists in education today. There would not be much time left for other subjects like history, geography, maths or music.

Finally, at thirteen or fourteen, some boys went on to higher education at the hands of a **rhetor**, who would teach him rhetoric, i.e. the art of public speaking. Girls were sometimes taught at the younger stages, but very few had higher education, and this reflects a certain amount about typical Roman attitudes towards women. Roman girls were not educated in the same way as boys, because women were generally expected to look after the family and the household. Roman boys, particularly those from wealthier families, spent longer in school because they were often expected to go into law and/or politics.

EXERCISE 14.6

1. Write out your timetable for today, and compare it with the lessons a child of your age might be having in ancient Rome.

2. Do you think that the writing implements used by Roman schoolchildren would be as easy to use as yours?

3. Try to find out about education in Britain 1850, for example, and see if it resembles Roman education more than our system today.

This picture shows a model of the ancient city of Rome. You may be able to spot some of the most famous buildings: the Circus Maximus and the Colosseum. Picture courtesy of F. Trefeu.

ADJECTIVES 15

An **adjective** is a word which describes a noun – a word like "big", "small", "pretty", "ugly".

In English these words never change, but if you are studying French you will know that in that language adjectives change their endings if a noun is **singular** or **plural**.

e.g.   le petit garçon
but   les petits garçons

So too if the noun is **feminine** other changes take place:

la petite fille
les petites filles

Most languages behave like this – in fact English is the exception – and in Latin adjectives change in **three** ways:

1)   **Number** – singular or plural
2)   **Gender** – masculine or feminine
3)   **Case** – nominative, accusative, etc.

You know how to recognise singular and plural (see Chapter 7), and also the various case endings (see Chapter 14). You now need to learn some rules for gender:

All nouns like puella are **feminine** unless they refer to men, i.e. **nauta**, **poeta**.

All nouns you have learnt like **servus**, **puer** and **ager** are **masculine**.

So in Latin an adjective will agree in **number, gender and case**:

e.g.   **magn<u>us</u> equus**   the big horse

              magn<u>a</u> hasta   the big spear

              magn<u>am</u> hastam video   I see the big spear

The above examples should be easy to follow, since the endings for both noun and adjective are the same. This is because adjectives like magnus have their **masculine** form like servus and their **feminine** form like puella.

These will therefore be easy to recognise, and here they are in full:

	SINGULAR		PLURAL	
	Masculine	**Feminine**	**Masculine**	**Feminine**
NOM	magn**us**	magn**a**	magn**ī**	magn**ae**
VOC	magn**e**	magn**a**	magn**ī**	magn**ae**
ACC	magn**um**	magn**am**	magn**ōs**	magn**ās**
GEN	magn**ī**	magn**ae**	magn**ōrum**	magn**ārum**
DAT	magn**ō**	magn**ae**	magn**īs**	magn**īs**
ABL	magn**ō**	magn**ā**	magn**īs**	magn**īs**

Here are some adjectives like **magnus** which should be learnt before doing the following exercises:

altus	high, deep
bonus	good
fessus	tired
iratus	angry
laetus	happy
malus	bad
novus	new
parvus	small

and mostly in the plural

>**multi**   many

In Latin adjectives usually come before the noun if they describe size or number:

e.g.   **magnus puer**   a big boy
            multi pueri   many boys
            quinque pueri   five boys

Otherwise they normally follow the noun:

>**puer bonus**   a good boy
>**puella fessa**   the tired girl

This word order is useful for you when you are writing in Latin, since you can carefully work out the noun ending (**number, gender and case**) and then make the adjective agree.

Note that **puer bonus** can mean either "**a** good boy" or "**the** good boy" – you need to decide which makes better sense as you translate (see note in Chapter 5).

EXERCISE 15.1

1.   multi servi magnam cenam parant.
2.   servi fessi agricolam iratum timent.
3.   nautae laeti ad oram insulae appropinquant.
4.   pueri mali murum agricolae delent.
5.   tabulam novam ad ludum porto.
6.   cur tu puellam parvam non iuvas, fili?
7.   femina bona pecuniam multis poetis dat.
8.   octo tauri in magno agro errant.
9.   magister bonus multos pueros docet.
10. regina irata muros altos oppugnat.

EXERCISE 15.2

1. The good girl is looking after the tired horse.
2. Many boys are walking towards the new wall.
3. The high river-bank frightens the little boy.
4. We are giving water to the tired slaves.
5. The naughty boys are fighting, and the angry schoolmaster is shouting.

There are a few adjectives which have a masculine form in **-er**, keeping the **-e** like **puer** or dropping it like **ager**.

Of the first sort is: **miser** miserable, wretched
and of the second: **pulcher** beautiful

	MASC	FEM	MASC	FEM
N/V	miser	misera	pulcher	pulchra
ACC	miser**um**	miser**am**	pulchr**um**	pulchr**am**

The rest of the case endings then follow the normal pattern as for **magnus**.

EXERCISE 15.3

1. servi miseri in agris laborant.
2. villam pulchram prope ripam videmus.
3. Gaius multos amicos ad cenam vocat.
4. dea pulchra nautas fessos iuvat.
5. magister laetus tres libros novos Marco dat.
6. pater incolis miseris damus.
7. magister multas fabulas pueris narrat.
8. servi fessi decem mensas in triclinium movent.
9. Publius equum novum amicis monstrat.
10. multi nuntii ad ianuam ludi appropinquant.

EXERCISE 15.4

Rewrite the following sentences putting the nouns, verbs and adjectives in the plural, and then translate into English.

1.   puer miser librum non habet.
2.   nauta puellam pulchram spectat.
3.   equus nuntii murum altum timet.
4.   magnus taurus puellam parvam terret.
5.   fabulam novam puero narro.

EXERCISE 15.5

1.   The beautiful girls are wandering through the garden.
2.   I am giving food to the wretched slaves.
3.   The angry goddess frightens the sailors.
4.   I am walking to school with many friends.
5.   How many new books do you have, (my) good friend?

EXERCISE 15.6

Write three Latin sentences to describe what is happening in the picture below. Try to use adjectives in your description.

Before translating the next exercise – a dialogue in a Roman school – it will be useful to learn the following new words:

salve(te)	hello!
taceo	I am silent
hodie	today
nunc	now
statim	immediately
tandem	at last
de + Abl	about

EXERCISE 15.7

magister:	salvete, pueri. intrate et sedete.
pueri:	salve, magister.
magister:	Marce, cur e ludo in viam ambulas? sede.
Marcus:	puellam pulchram in via specto, magister.
magister:	intra ludum statim, Marce, et sede.
Marcus:	ego nunc sedeo.
magister:	Publi, cur tu clamas? tace.
Publius:	ego non clamo, magister. ego taceo.
magister:	Quinte, cur tabulam non habes?
Quintus:	tabulam Marci nunc habeo, magister.
magister:	o Marce, cur cum Quinto pugnas? Quinte, da tabulam Marco statim. tacete, pueri.
pueri:	tacemus, magister.
magister:	tandem vos tacetis. fabulasne amatis? ego, pueri, fabulam de Romulo et Remo hodie narro.

EXERCISE 15.8

1. At last the boys are silent.
2. Today I am watching the poet's house.
3. The schoolmaster immediately enters the school with the boys.
4. Hello, Gaius. Why are you hiding the books?
5. Father is now telling a story about a beautiful girl.

EXERCISE 15.9

1.   Explain the meaning of the following English words,
     and show how they derive from Latin:

     altitude   irate   mural   taciturn

2.   Find English derivatives from the following Latin words,
     and write a sentence for each to show its meaning
     clearly:

     liber   magnus   novus   vir

ROMULUS AND REMUS

The schoolmaster may well have told the story of **Romulus
and Remus** to his pupils. You may remember they were
mentioned in Chapter 2, and you must bear in mind that this
was a story to the Romans also. It therefore belongs more to
the realms of legend than to fact. What is perhaps interesting is
that the Romans living many centuries afterwards liked to think
that this is the way their great imperial city had begun.

There was a very nasty king in Italy called **Amulius** – a typical
"wicked uncle" character! He seized the throne from his brother,
and had his brother's sons murdered while making his brother's
daughter promise that she would never marry and have children.

However, she later gave birth to twin boys and declared that
their father was none other than **Mars**, the god of war. Whether
this was true or not, wicked Amulius had her flung into prison
and ordered the boys to be drowned in the river Tiber. By
chance the river had overflowed its banks. The men who were
sent to drown the babies left them in a container in the flood
water near the river, thinking that this would be enough to do
the dreadful deed.

A little while later a **she-wolf** came down from the nearby hills
to have a drink and heard the pitiful crying of the babies. She
fed them and was nursing them, when the king's shepherd
came along. He took pity on these poor unfortunates, and
carried them home for his wife to look after.

So the boys grew up in humble surroundings to become fine
young men. The shepherd had always thought that there had
been something remarkable about their rescue, and, knowing
the story of the king ordering his nephews to be drowned,
began to suspect that these two were those very boys.
Therefore the shepherd at last decided to tell the truth, and
Romulus and Remus decided to found a new town on the very
spot where they had been left to drown and then rescued.

However, once again jealousy and rivalry destroyed noble
plans. Just as their grandfather had quarrelled with his brother
Amulius, so Romulus and Remus also quarrelled – over which
was the older twin! If any of you are twins, you had better
watch out!

There are several stories about their quarrel. The most common
is that while the town was being built Remus laughed at his
brother's efforts and jumped over the half-built walls. Romulus
is then said to have killed him in a fit of temper and he thus
became sole ruler of the new city which was named after him –
Roma.

EXERCISE 15.10

1. Why do you think that this story appealed to the Romans living several centuries after it supposedly happened?

2. Do you think that this is a good story to describe the founding of Rome?

3. Can you think of any other story, fact or fiction, where brothers quarrel?

Mosaics were popular decorations in ancient Rome, and were made by piecing together many tiny fragments of coloured rocks and stones to build up a picture. This one from a Sicilian villa, the Piazza Armerina, shows men using dogs and spears to hunt for wild boar. Picture courtesy of Editions Lidis.

THE VERB "SUM"

16

In Latin, as in English and other languages, there are several verbs which are highly irregular. These are usually the most common verbs, such as the verb "to be".

Here is the verb sum meaning "I am", and note how even in English this verb does not follow the normal pattern:

sum	I am
es	You are
est	He/she/it is
sumus	We are
estis	You are
sunt	They are

You will see from the highlighted endings that apart from the **-m** of **sum**, the other endings are the same as those you have learnt for **amo** and **video** (see Chapter 8).

When the personal pronouns are included you will see how close **sum** is to its French equivalent.

ego sum	je suis
tu es	tu es
ille est	il est
illa est	elle est
nos sumus	nous sommes
vos estis	vous êtes
illi sunt	ils sont
illae sunt	elles sont

The verb **sum** is used, just as in English, with other nouns or adjectives – always agreeing in the **nominative** case.

> **ego sum magister**
> I am a schoolmaster

> **pueri sunt laeti**
> The boys are happy

Note that unlike other Latin verbs **sum** does not necessarily come at the end of a sentence.

EXERCISE 16.1

1. ripa est alta.
2. servi miseri sunt.
3. hodie fessi sumus.
4. filia agricolae est puella bona.
5. puerorum tabulae sunt novae.
6. ego sum laetus, cur tu es miser?
7. Tullia tandem laeta est.
8. nuntius reginae est fessus.
9. quis est Publius? nonne est filius poetae?
10. salve, Marce. cur iratus es?

EXERCISE 16.2

1. The slaves are now tired.
2. The queen's daughter is a small girl.
3. The poet's new house is big.
4. Why are you happy today, Quintus?
5. We are good boys, sir, but Marcus is naughty.

est and **sunt** can also be used to mean "there is/are".

> **est magna casa prope viam.**
> There is a large house near the road.

> **sunt tres tauri in agro.**
> There are three bulls in the field.

EXERCISE 16.3

1.   est nuntius in atrio.
2.   sunt octo epistolae in mensa.
3.   sunt multae casae novae prope ripam.
4.   cur Marcus non est in ludo hodie?
5.   quot tauri in agro sunt?
6.   est femina irata in via.
7.   est magnus murus prope villam Tulliae.
8.   sunt quinque puellae in horto.
9.   ubi est soror Quinti? estne in culina?
10. cur es laetus hodie, Gai? habesne equum novum?

EXERCISE 16.4

1.   There are five boys in the water.
2.   There is a new master in the school.
3.   There is a large dinner on the table.
4.   How many slaves are in the kitchen?
5.   Where is Gaius? Is he in the house?

Before translating the next exercise, it will be useful to learn the following words:

deinde	then
diu	for a long time
quod	because
saepe	often
subito	suddenly

EXERCISE 16.5

Marcus in Campania habitat. Campania est in Italia. pater Marci est agricola. pater et filius in agris saepe laborant. hodie fessi sunt, quod diu laborant. vesper appropinquat, sed subito magnus taurus ad agricolam et filium festinat. taurus puerum oppugnat. pater clamat, et filium miserum iuvat. deinde taurus cibum prope ripam videt, et a puero festinat. pater nunc laetus est. puerum curat, et pater et filius ad casam ambulant.

in casa mater et filia agricolam et puerum exspectant. cenam parant. cibum et vinum in culinam portant. nunc mater laeta est, quod vir et filius tandem appropinquant.

EXERCISE 16.6

Write two Latin sentences to describe what is happening in the picture below. Try to use adjectives in your description.

Take care when translating into Latin between the use of "is/are" with a noun or adjective which requires **sum**, and the use of "is/are" as part of another verb (see Chapter 5)

So	The boy IS big **puer EST magnus**
but	The boy IS SWIMMING **puer NATAT**
and	The boys ARE happy **pueri SUNT laeti**
but	The boys ARE FIGHTING **pueri PUGNANT**

EXERCISE 16.7

1. The boys are often in the garden.
2. The farmer's bull is large.
3. Suddenly the girl is hurrying out of the house.
4. The wretched slaves are working for a long time in the fields.
5. The schoolmaster is angry, because the naughty boys are shouting.

LIFE IN THE COUNTRY

The little passage above may or may not be describing a typical day in the life of country folk.

Campania was indeed a district in **Southern Italy**, and even today life for those living on the land is not always easy. In about AD 100 a typical Roman farmer may have had enough money to own one or two slaves (see Chapter 9), but many would have done all the work themselves, aided by members of their family.

A farmer had to grow enough to feed his family, and perhaps have some left over to sell or exchange for other goods at the market. Work was certainly long and arduous, and farmers (as indeed they do today) had to get up early and work until late, especially during the summer months when daylight was longest. However, if the weather became too hot and dry, they might have rested, but they would have to water their land if at all possible. In mid-winter also, if the weather became too severe, farmers had a brief break from daily work.

Grain and fruit were grown to provide the food, vines to make wine, and olives to provide olive oil – for which Mediterranean countries are still rightly famous. The olive oil was used not only for cooking, but also to make soap and to provide oil for lamps.

The poet **Virgil** (see Chapter 4) wrote a poem in four books about farming and the countryside, aiming to encourage the Romans to stop fighting over their land, and to look after it. This poem is called the **Georgics** (*ge-ōrgos* is the Greek word for "farmer"), and one of the books is devoted to bee-keeping, another possible source of income for farmers. However, he was writing as much for the rich landowners who owned vast estates and had countless slaves to work for them (see the **villa** in Chapter 6), as for the small independent farmer. Yet he does give a good picture of life for the ordinary farmer, as in this passage:

> "Meanwhile the farmer has been cutting apart the ground with his crooked plough. From here comes his year's work, from here comes the way to feed his country and his little grandsons, from here food for his herds of oxen and his worthy cattle. He has no rest, but the season is either full of fruit or with the growing flocks or with the sheaves of Ceres' corn, and the crops load the furrows and burst the barns."

EXERCISE 16.8

1.   If you live in the country, compare the lifestyle of a modern farmer with one living in Roman times.

2.   In many parts of the world farming methods are no more advanced than those of Roman times. Why do you think this is so?

VOCABULARY

LATIN-ENGLISH

a, ab + Abl	from
ad + Acc	to, towards
aedifico	I build
ager	field
agricola	farmer
altus	high, deep
ambulo	I walk
amicus	friend
amo	I love, like
appropinquo	I approach
atrium	entrance-hall
aqua	water
bonus	good
canto	I sing
casa	house
celo	I hide
cena	dinner
cibus	food
clamo	I shout
contra + Acc	against
culina	kitchen
cum + Abl	with
cur?	why?
curo	I look after
de + Abl	about (i.e. concerning)
dea	goddess
decem	ten
deinde	then
deleo	I destroy

deus	god
do	I give
doceo	I teach
duo	two
e, ex + Abl	out of
ego	I
epistola	letter
equus	horse
erro	I wander
et	and
exspecto	I wait for
fabula	story
femina	woman
fessus	tired
festino	I hurry
filia	daughter
filius	son
frater	brother
gladius	sword
habeo	I have
habito	I live (in)
hasta	spear
hodie	today
hortus	garden
ianua	door
illa	she
ille	he
illi, illae	they
in + Abl	in, on
in + Acc	into, on to
incola	inhabitant
insula	island, block of flats
intro	I enter
ira	anger
iratus	angry

itaque	and so, therefore
iuvo	I help
laboro	I work
laetus	happy
laudo	I praise
lectus	couch, bed
liber	book
libertus	freedman
ludus	school
magister	schoolmaster
magnus	big, large, great
malus	bad
maneo	I stay, wait
mater	mother
mensa	table
miser	miserable, wretched
moneo	I warn, advise
monstro	I show, point out
moveo	I move
multi	many
murus	wall
narro	I tell
nato	I swim
nauta	sailor
navigo	I sail
-ne?	?
non	not
nonne?	surely?
nos	we
novem	nine
novus	new
num?	surely not?
nunc	now
nuntius	messenger, message
octo	eight
oppugno	I attack

ora	shore
paro	I prepare
parvus	small, little
pater	father
pecunia	money
per + Acc	through
poeta	poet
porto	I carry
prope + Acc	near
puella	girl
puer	boy
pugno	I fight
pulcher	beautiful
quattuor	four
quid?	what?
quinque	five
quis?	who?
quod	because
quot?	how many?
regina	queen
respondeo	I reply, answer
rex	king
ripa	river-bank
saepe	often
sagitta	arrow
saluto	I greet
salve(te)	hello!, greetings!
sed	but
sedeo	I sit
semper	always
septem	seven
servo	I keep safe
servus	slave
sex	six
silva	wood
soror	sister

specto	I look at
statim	immediately
sto	I stand
subito	suddenly
tabula	writing-tablet
taceo	I am silent
tandem	at last
taurus	bull
teneo	I hold
terreo	I frighten
timeo	I fear, am afraid of
tres	three
triclinium	dining-room
tu	you (singular)
ubi?	where?
unus	one
ventus	wind
vesper	evening
via	road, way
video	I see
villa	country-house
vinum	wine
vir	man, husband
voco	I call
vos	you (plural)

ENGLISH-LATIN

against	**contra + acc**
advise, I	**moneo**
always	**semper**
and	**et**
and so	**itaque**
anger	**ira**
angry	**iratus**
approach, I	**appropinquo**
arrow	**sagitta**
attack, I	**oppugno**
bad	**malus**
beautiful	**pulcher**
because	**quod**
bed	**lectus**
big	**magnus**
book	**liber**
boy	**puer**
brother	**frater**
build, I	**aedifico**
bull	**taurus**
but	**sed**
call, I	**voco**
carry, I	**porto**
couch	**lectus**
daughter	**filia**
destroy, I	**deleo**
dinner	**cena**
door	**ianua**
eight	**octo**
enter, I	**intro**
evening	**vesper**
farmer	**agricola**

father	**pater**
fear, I	**timeo**
field	**ager**
fight, I	**pugno**
five	**quinque**
food	**cibus**
four	**quattuor**
freedman	**libertus**
friend	**amicus**
frighten, I	**terreo**
from	**a, ab + abl**
garden	**hortus**
girl	**puella**
give, I	**do**
god	**deus**
goddess	**dea**
good	**bonus**
greet, I	**saluto**
happy	**laetus**
have, I	**habeo**
help, I	**iuvo**
hide, I	**celo**
high	**altus**
hold, I	**teneo**
horse	**equus**
house	**casa**
how many?	**quot?**
hurry, I	**festino**
I	**ego**
into, on to	**in + acc**
in, on	**in + abl**
inhabitant	**incola**
island	**insula**
keep safe, I	**servo**
kitchen	**culina**

large	**magnus**
letter	**epistola**
like, I	**amo**
little	**parvus**
live, I	**habito**
look after, I	**curo**
look at, I	**specto**
love, I	**amo**
man	**vir**
many	**multi**
message	**nuntius**
messenger	**nuntius**
miserable	**miser**
money	**pecunia**
mother	**mater**
move, I	**moveo**
near	**prope + acc**
new	**novus**
nine	**novem**
not	**non**
now	**nunc**
often	**saepe**
one	**unus**
out of	**e, ex + abl**
poet	**poeta**
praise, I	**laudo**
prepare, I	**paro**
queen	**regina**
reply, I	**respondeo**
river-bank	**ripa**
road	**via**
sail, I	**navigo**
sailor	**nauta**

school	**ludus**
schoolmaster	**magister**
see, I	**video**
seven	**septem**
shore	**ora**
shout, I	**clamo**
show, I	**monstro**
sing, I	**canto**
sister	**soror**
sit, I	**sedeo**
six	**sex**
slave	**servus**
small	**parvus**
son	**filius**
spear	**hasta**
stand, I	**sto**
stay, I	**maneo**
story	**fabula**
suddenly	**subito**
surely?	**nonne?**
surely not?	**num?**
swim, I	**nato**
sword	**gladius**
table	**mensa**
teach, I	**doceo**
tell, I	**narro**
ten	**decem**
then	**deinde**
three	**tres**
through	**per + acc**
tired	**fessus**
to, towards	**ad + acc**
today	**hodie**
two	**duo**
wait, I	**maneo**
walk, I	**ambulo**
wall	**murus**
wander, I	**erro**

warn, I	**moneo**
watch, I	**specto**
water	**aqua**
we	**nos**
what?	**quid?**
where?	**ubi?**
who?	**quis?**
why?	**cur?**
wind	**ventus**
with	**cum + abl**
woman	**femina**
wood	**silva**
work, I	**laboro**
wretched	**miser**
you (plural)	**vos**
you (singular)	**tu**

LATIN-BASED WEB SITES

Below is a collection of some of the most useful web pages that we found in a search for sites that concentrate on ancient Rome and the Latin language. Please bear in mind that the World Wide Web is an ever-changing entity, and that before long, many of these sites may move or be taken off the Net. However, we do feel that there is a huge amount of useful information, activities, maps, and teaching resources of all sorts, so we have sifted through the rubbish to produce what we hope is a list of some of the most interesting Latin-orientated web sites on the Net.

http://www.home.ch/~spaw1087/orgy/index.html
Everything you ever wanted to know about the ancient art of Roman cooking. Includes Apicius' recipes.

http://www.ancientsites.com
A large and impressive site with a wide range of pictures, computer simulations and activities relating to ancient Rome – allows you to become a citizen of ancient Rome.

http://www.geocities.com/Athens/Styx/9585/formum.html
A wide range of links and information regarding all things classical. Also teaching materials.

http://www.geocities.com/Athens/Styx/1790/index.html
Latin Teach site: forum for exchanging ideas and experiences with other teachers. Includes a wide range of teaching resources.

http://www.tlg.uci.edu/~tlg/index/resources.html
Electronic Resources for Classicists – fairly self-explanatory.

http://www.geocities.com/Athens/Crete/4634/
Some useful teaching resources.

http://www.slu.edu/colleges/AS/languages/tchmat.html
A good resource for texts in Latin.

http://www.people.Virginia.EDU/~kk2e/Latin/
A variety of texts in Latin.

**http://www.ukans.edu/history/index/europe/ancient_rome/E/
Roman/Texts/secondary/SMIGRA/home.html**
An interesting selection of articles on aspects of Roman life.

http://www.novaroma.org/main.html
Source of information on life and culture in ancient Rome. Main
emphasis is on religion.

**http://www.ukans.edu/history/index/europe/ancient_rome/E/
Roman/RomanSites*/home.html**
A wide variety of Latin texts, and also a large number of useful links
to other Roman web sites.

http://www.fh-augsburg.de/~harsch/augusta.html
A range of texts in Latin.

http://patriot.net/~lillard/cp/
A variety of Latin texts, and links to Latin-orientated web sites.

http://ancienthistory.miningco.com
Wide range of information on all aspects of life in ancient Rome.

http://www.orient.uw.edu.pl/~conradus/latina.html
A variety of Latin texts.

http://www.togatees.com
Site containing Latin witticisms.

http://www.rmc.edu/~gdaugher/elem.html
Information on Ancient Mediterranean civilisations, including a lot of
Roman art.

http://wings.buffalo.edu/AandL/Maecenas/
Large collection of photographs of Roman buildings, architecture,
ruins, etc.

http://www.txclassics.org/fungame.html#top
Some amusing games to help teach Latin.

http://www.txclassics.org/links.htm
Page of links to all sorts of Latin-orientated web pages.

http://www.novaroma.org/via_romana/names.html
Explanation of system of Romans' names.

http://www.usask.ca/classics/CourseNotes/RomanName.html
More detailed account of Roman nomenclature.

http://www.geocities.com/~magisstra
Latin grammar including history of the language, derivations, etc.

http://www.umich.edu/~acleague
Web site for the American Classical League: Latin texts, information, teaching advice and resources, pictures etc.

http://www.nd.edu/~archives/latgramm.htm
Latin grammar aid, including dictionary.

http://www.emory.edu/CARLOS/ODYSSEY
Easily digestible information on daily life and culture in the Ancient Roman Empire. Includes pictures.

http://www.virginia.edu/~libarts/classics.htm
Good variety of pictures of Olympian gods, from Roman through to modern art.

http://www.jmiller.demon.co.uk/
Maps of the Roman Empire, Italy and Forum.

http://www.cco.net/~jcurtis/latin.htm
Latin mottoes and phrases.

http://www.geocities.com/Athens/Crete/4634/latin.html
Excellent variety of teaching resources, including grammar, texts, quizzes, games, songs in Latin, etc.

http://homepages.iol.ie/~coolmine/typ/romans/intro.html
Easily digestible general information on history and culture of Romans.

http://www.pen.k12.va.us/Anthology/Pav/Classics/Forum.shtml
Educational information and forum for discussion.

http://artemis.austinc.edu/acad/cml/rcape/vcrc/
Wide variety of Roman coins.

http://www.geocities.com/~i_claudius/
Pictures, magazine, chat rooms based on Latin and Roman times.

http://www.geocities.com/Athens/Forum/6946/
A huge variety of information, virtual tour and pictures showing places and people from Roman history and mythology.

http://library.advanced.org/11402/home_intro.html
Easily understood, varied, done by school kids. Lots of info, quizzes, etc. Fun and informative.

iam.classics.unc.edu
Interactive Ancient Mediterranean: good maps, etc.